Building Self-Esteem in Children and
Teens Who Are Adopted or Fostered

of related interest

Helping Children to Build Self-Esteem
A Photocopiable Activities Book
Second Edition
Deborah M. Plummer
ISBN 978 1 84310 488 9
eISBN 978 1 84642 609 4

Self-Esteem Games for Children
Deborah M. Plummer
Illustrated by Jane Serrurier
ISBN 978 1 84310 424 7
eISBN 978 1 84642 574 5

Attaching in Adoption
Practical Tools for Today's Parents
Deborah D. Gray
ISBN 978 1 84905 890 2
eISBN 978 0 85700 606 6

Attaching through Love, Hugs and Play
Simple Strategies to Help Build
Connections with Your Child
Deborah D. Gray
ISBN 978 1 84905 939 8
eISBN 978 0 85700 753 7

The Foster Parenting Manual
A Practical Guide to Creating a
Loving, Safe and Stable Home
John DeGarmo
ISBN 978 1 84905 956 5
eISBN 978 0 85700 795 7

A Different Home
A New Foster Child's Story
John DeGarmo and Kelly DeGarmo
ISBN 978 1 84905 987 9
eISBN 978 0 85700 897 8

Keeping Foster Children Safe Online
Positive Strategies to Prevent Cyberbullying,
Inappropriate Contact and Other Digital Dangers
John DeGarmo
ISBN 978 1 84905 973 2
eISBN 978 0 85700 862 6

Building Self-Esteem in Children and Teens Who Are Adopted or Fostered

Dr. Sue Cornbluth

Foreword by Nyleen Shaw

Jessica Kingsley *Publishers*
London and Philadelphia

Transcript in Foreword is reproduced with kind permission from Brad Segall from CBS Radio, Philadelphia.

First published in 2014
by Jessica Kingsley Publishers
73 Collier Street
London N1 9BE, UK
and
400 Market Street, Suite 400
Philadelphia, PA 19106, USA

www.jkp.com

Library of Congress Cataloging in Publication Data
Cornbluth, Sue.
  Building self-esteem in children and teens who are adopted or fostered / Sue Cornbluth ; foreword by
Nyleen Shaw.
      pages cm
  Includes bibliographical references and index.
  ISBN 978-1-84905-466-9 (alk. paper)
1. Adopted children. 2. Foster children. 3. Self-esteem in children. 4. Self-esteem in adolescence.
5. Child psychology. 6. Child rearing. I. Title.
  HV875.C676 2014
  155.4'182--dc23
2014001036

British Library Cataloguing in Publication Data
A CIP catalogue record for this book is available from the British Library

ISBN 978 1 84905 466 9
eISBN 978 0 85700 844 2

Printed and bound in the United States

To Darrin, Jacob and Lindsay, my life and my world.

And to my mother, who taught me the meaning of the importance of being an advocate for others. And to my father, who taught me never to give up on myself.

To Nyleen, for teaching me through her inner strength that a child can heal from abuse.

And to every child throughout the world who has been in foster care or adopted. You have the right to feel wanted, needed and loved. Every child should grow up in a forever home and every parent and professional caring for these children should be given the "tools" to help fostered and adopted children succeed in a world where they have been dealt extremely unfair circumstances. This book is my gift to all of you.

CONTENTS

Foreword

Nyleen Shaw and Sue Cornbluth

I finally got my chance to tell my truth one night on the radio. Dr. Sue told me that someday I would be able to tell my story about growing up in foster care and what Dr. Sue says, she delivers. It was a cold night in December of 2011 and I met Dr. Sue at the CBS studio in Philadelphia. She looked exactly as I remembered, and greeted me with a big smile on her face. I had not seen her since 2000, when I went off to college, something I never thought that I would accomplish, coming from where I came from.

It had been 11 years since Dr. Sue and I had seen each other but it felt like yesterday. Throughout those 11 years, she would often check in with me by email to see how I was doing. I really appreciated it more than she will ever know. Dr. Sue helped me to believe in myself when no one else did. She told me I could be someone in this world, no matter what happened to me. She taught me to have inner strength and gave me the ability to trust and believe that not all people would hurt me.

When Dr. Sue asked me to write the foreword to her book, I was shocked but so grateful. This would be my second chance to share our interview with other people and let the world know that foster children are not "damaged" children. In fact, we are just like other children who often do not understand why we are treated in ways that we do not understand. We are looking for love and compassion just like all children. What we don't want is to be labeled and stigmatized because we grew up in a system that we did not deserve to be in.

I hope that what I am about to share with you changes your view about abused and neglected foster children and gives you faith that the work you are doing with us makes a big difference in our lives if it is done right.

This is the excerpt from my interview on CBS Radio:

I was six years old and up to that point my mom was off drugs. We would play, go to the zoo. We were a family then. Life was normal for me at that point. When I was six my mother was also introduced to drugs, cocaine and basically from there things went downhill. There were times when our aunts and uncles would give us presents and the next day they would be gone and my mom would sell them. There were times when we would get beat for what we thought was nothing. We would say, "Mom we are hungry," and the next thing you know we would get beat. Any little tiny thing at school, we would get beat. It became a normal thing for us to get beat. We knew depending on what kind of mood my mom would come in the house what was going to happen that day. I didn't have a dad and there was five of us kids in the house. I was the third child of five children. My mom mentally and physically abused all of us.

Me and my siblings were not placed into foster care until I was nine. But starting at six my school started making reports to the department of human services because we would go to school and we all looked neglected. We were hungry all the time and we wore the same clothes a lot and our hair was a mess. Neighbors too were making reports and our relatives. My brothers and sisters and I were not removed from my mom right away. It takes time when you're dealing with the system.

There was like a system going on in my house with my mom and the world needs to know about it. Parents and families that know that they are doing wrong try to cover it up. There is a secret society going on within the household. You just know not to speak about the abuse to others. So when the case managers were coming to check on me and my siblings, we all lied about my mother abusing us and not taking care of us. For me, it just got to a point where I just could not take it anymore. I felt like I got it worse from my mom than my siblings and I just wanted out. A couple of times when the caseworkers came I told the truth because I wanted out. My mom beat me for that. I just figured if I kept lying to the caseworkers they would never help us. So to me telling the truth was my way out of the situation and that is how I got placed into the foster care system. However, we did not go to foster care right away; my brother's grandmother stepped in initially and took all of us in. They call that kinship care. Her and her husband did not have enough money to care for all of us as time went by. I was about eight at the time. Eventually we were all split up, except for my youngest brother who stayed with his grandmother.

Through all of the abuse and the five foster homes I was in, I still had dreams and desires to be someone. This came from me looking at my biological family members and telling myself that I wanted the complete opposite of their lives. I looked around the neighborhood I grew up in and looked at the people every day and no one had any accomplishments. The big turning point for me was when I heard that a cousin of mine was going to college. Finally, I thought, someone in my life is going to do something positive with her life and I thought that is what I want to do too. From that moment on I knew that from there, education had to be my way out. So, that is when I began to focus on school, books, reading and athletics. The longer I could stay in school, the less time I had to spend at home. After school, when everyone was happy about going home, I was happy about staying at school. It was my way of protecting myself.

Later with the help of Dr. Sue's belief in me, I graduated with a degree in criminal justice/psychology with a minor in English from West Chester University. I have been a social worker for the last three years helping kids like I was helped.

I want people to know that it is never too late to heal from being abused. I was a child put into the system because of what my mom did and it is always going to affect my life. Being separated from your parents stays with you forever. It is always a part of you and will be there. You don't forget your mother telling you that you are the biggest mistake she ever had. Now, in my twenties, I can forgive her but I want people to know I do not forget the pain and the abuse she put me through.

What helped me to heal from what had happened to me was that I had some great foster parents who would not let me sit around and see myself as a victim. They would not let me say to myself, "Woe is me." Also, when I met Dr. Sue, she helped me change and turn my whole thought process around on the fact that I could not only have goals but actually accomplish them. I thought I could never accomplish a goal because I was a foster child and we had stereotypes placed on us that we would just be a statistic of the system. You know, end up in jail, pregnant or homeless. No one before Dr. Sue ever validated my feelings before that: "It's okay to feel the way you feel but now what are you going to do about it?" Meeting Dr. Sue helped me actually turn my feelings into positive actions because she believed in me. She would always say, "It's okay to be angry but how are you going to channel it in a way in which you are benefiting from it and going to develop and grow from it?" I would always hear her voice in my head over the years saying, "What you are doing every day by thinking positive is making a better life for yourself. Where you came from matters but it is not all of you. You have the power to shape your life."

That foster family and Dr. Sue became my support system and I needed one. I learned that being a foster child was not really who I was. It was a part of who I was but not all of me. I had a choice about my destiny. The most important thing I can say, is that I healed from my relationship with Dr. Sue and my foster family. It's the relationship, people. It's the relationship that helps us kids out.

Nyleen Shaw
Foster care survivor and child advocate

ACKNOWLEDGMENTS

This book is something that I have always wanted to write but I never seemed to find the time to do so. I'm so glad that I finally found the time. For years, foster and adoptive parents and professionals have asked me to put all of my suggestions down on paper. I am so pleased that I have finally accomplished this for them and the children.

I must first thank my husband Darrin, my partner in life and in parenting. Your support for my career over the years has meant the world to me. You have encouraged me every step of the way and have taught me never to give up on my dreams. As a father to our children, you are truly amazing. Your commitment to their hopes and dreams is inspiring to watch. I am so happy and grateful that I have you to share my life with.

To the most important and amazing children any mother could ever have, Jacob and Lindsay. You light up my world every single day with your laughter, smiles and your loving ways. I did not know how much I could love until the both of you came into my life. I am so proud to be your mother. I know that it was not easy this last year for you both as I had to take time away from you to write this book. You were both so understanding and I thank you.

To my parents who have encouraged me since I was a young girl to follow my dreams and become whatever I desired. Mom, you always told me that whenever things went wrong "I could still come out on top" and you were right. You have taught me over the years how to stand up for myself and to fight for others. You are the person who taught me how to advocate for parents and kids to the best of my ability. Dad, what would we have if we did not do things to the best of our ability? Not much, I guess. You have taught me that whatever I did in life, I should give 100 percent. At times growing up, I resented that but as an adult I appreciate it more than you know. I would not be where I am today without you instilling that philosophy in me. Thank you for that. I also want to thank both of my parents for teaching me that parents are not perfect and are capable of making mistakes. I also want to thank my entire extended family and my fans for your dedicated support to my work.

I want to thank my first supervisor in the foster care field, Judith Feldman, for giving me the opportunity to get my feet wet in a field I knew nothing about: foster care. I thank you for allowing me to think outside the box when it came to helping fostered and adopted children in the way I thought best. I am extremely grateful.

Thank you to my incredible and dedicated publicist, Debra Goetz, for helping me to become a nationally recognized expert in foster care and child abuse. You have been an instrumental part of helping me reach my dreams. We make an amazing team and I look forward to the future.

Thank you to Brad Segall of KYW News Radio, CBS Radio and "The Philadelphia Agenda" in Philadelphia, PA for giving me a forum to discuss foster care and adoptive issues. I am most grateful to you for giving Nyleen a voice. You are a dynamic broadcaster and a dear friend. Also, thank you to Anzio Williams, News Director at NBC10 Philadelphia and to Lynn Doyle, host of Comcast's "It's Your Call" for giving me an opportunity to bring the issues around child abuse to the forefront of the news.

I would also like to thank Stephen Jones, commissioning editor at Jessica Kingsley Publishers, for asking me to write this book. Sometimes you need a push to make it happen. Thank you for believing in my work and for allowing me the freedom to write in the way that I can best express myself.

To all of the amazing foster and adoptive parents who have allowed me to enter their lives as their trainer. I have learned so much from all of you about how to parent fostered and adopted children. I want you all to know how much I admire you for helping and sacrificing your lives to shape these children's lives. You are amazing human beings.

To Nyleen Shaw, the strongest survivor I have ever met. You are an inspiration to me and all foster children around the world. It is because of you that I decided to write this book.

Finally, to all of the fostered and adopted children and teens I have counseled over the years. You are such incredible, strong and courageous people. You have all inspired me to help as many children as I can in this world. You are true survivors. Stay strong and never give up on your dreams.

Introduction

I was eight years old the night my parents had a terrible fight. My mother grabbed her keys and ran so fast out of the house. I remember crying and screaming. I ran after her but my father stopped me. I watched as she jumped into her car and drove away. I sat on the oatmeal-colored carpeted steps in the hallway with tears rolling down my face. My body was filled with sheer panic as tears rolled down my small red cheeks. I couldn't catch my breath. My body was frozen like an ice cube.

Did I mention I was only eight years old? It was in that moment that I feared that I would never see my mother again. My father tried to calm me down by saying, "She will be back, don't worry. She just needs to blow some steam off." I tuned out his voice. I did not care what he was saying; I was worried that I would never see my mom again. Why did he have to yell at her? Why did he make her leave me? For one hour, I sat on those steps, staring and crying for my mother to return. I never took my eyes off the door, not even for a second.

The first hour passed and there was no sign of my mother. I did not leave the steps. I sat and waited. It was as if my body was glued to the carpet and nothing was going to lift me up until my mom came through the front door. The second hour passed and still no sign of my mother. I felt panic, alone, helpless and afraid. Fifteen minutes later I heard the key turn in the door and she appeared. She looked as though she had been crying for days. It was in that moment that my panic dissolved and sheer relief overcame me. I rose from the steps and ran as fast as I could to give her a hug.

My mother came back and never left me again. I was one of the lucky kids.

She held me in her arms. I felt relieved, angry and scared all at the same time. As we sat together in my room, she promised me that she would never leave me again. She said leaving was the "wrong" thing to do and that a mother should never leave her child even if she is upset. I hugged my mom so tight that night. I think I couldn't breathe.

Following that night, I thought about my mother leaving me for days on end. I wondered when it would happen again. What if my parents had another fight? Would I ever see my mother again? As time passed, my parents had more fights; however, my mother kept her promise and did not leave.

Due to my mother's consistent response to me over time, my fear decreased. I learned through time that no marriage is perfect and that mothers and fathers can make mistakes and also keep their word.

The real question looking back now at 40 years old is, "Why should an eight-year-old have to be worried about their mother ever leaving and coming back?" Aren't parents supposed to take care of their children and never leave them? One would think so, right?

The truth is that there are many mothers and fathers who walk out the door every day and do not return. These children are not as lucky as I once was. In September 2012, there were an estimated 399,546 children in the foster care system (Child Welfare Information Gateway, 2013); 115,000 children are available for adoption, but nearly 40% of these children will wait more than three years in foster care before being adopted (Congressional Coalition on Adoption Institute, 2014). In addition, there are hundreds of thousands of orphans throughout the world. All of these children need "forever homes" with supportive parents to become successful individuals.

The number one concern children face when coming into foster care is learning to bond with new caretakers. The second main concern is their level of self-worth. Attachment and self-esteem are the two most critical aspects to healing from the trauma the children experienced prior to being placed into foster care. Notice how I did not mention changing the child's behaviors as one of the main concerns. This is for a very important reason. Negative behaviors stem from unresolved emotional issues. Behaviors do not form on their own. Behaviors are fueled by unresolved emotions about circumstances. Abandonment, abuse and low self-worth are just a few of the emotional causes of what many people call "bad behaviors."

Almost every fostered or adopted child that I have worked with over the last 15 years has struggled with self-esteem issues. "Why is this?" you may ask. Well, think about these two scenarios for a minute:

One day you are living at home with your biological family and the next day you are living in a strange place with strange people. You are ripped away from what you consider to be a "normal" family life and you do not understand why this is happening. All the social worker keeps telling you is that this is in the best interest of keeping you safe. All you want to do is go home but you can't. You feel trapped and helpless.

You were adopted as a baby but now you are nine years old and you feel different from all the other kids. Your adoptive parents told you about being adopted but you didn't really know what that meant until you had to fill out a paper that read, "Who are your birth parents?" You begin to think that you are "different" and that you do not fit in with the other kids. You feel depressed, rejected and abandoned. You begin to wonder if your adopted parents will leave you too.

Now ask yourself: "How would I feel in these circumstances?"

Note: Real names are not used in this book to protect privacy.

CHAPTER 1

Fostered and Adopted Children and Teens Struggle with Self-Esteem

People ask me all the time why I became so interested in helping fostered and adopted children and their families find a way to relate to each other in a safe and respected way. It is because of my experience when I was eight years old. The truth is that if my mother had never run out of the house that day when I was eight, I might never have found my passion for this work. It was in that moment that I felt sheer panic and total helplessness. It was in that moment that I understood what it could have felt like never to see my mother again. It was in those two hours and 15 minutes that I felt complete abandonment. It was in that moment that I realized that I never wanted another child to feel that pain. It was 20 years later, when I was 28 years old, that I walked into a foster care facility to provide outpatient therapy to hundreds of children and decided that helping these children fulfil their given potential would be my life's work.

I never shared the story of when I was eight years old until I was asked to write this book. I thought that it would embarrass my parents. However, I have learned throughout my life that sharing my authenticity is important in helping children and adults heal from trauma. It helps people to know that they are not alone in their pain.

I was never a foster child and I am not adopted. I would never compare my experience to a fostered or adopted child's life or journey. That would be unfair. What I can say is that the feeling of helplessness I had years ago continues to live on in hundreds of thousands of children who do not have the opportunity to live every day with their biological parents. Despite the loss of their parents, family and possessions, I believe that they can live successful lives. I have seen it with my own eyes. This success, however, begins with you, the professionals, foster parents and adoptive parents. You are the vehicle of change in these children's lives.

Last year, while providing training to foster parents at a local agency, I learned the true power of the statement: "You are the vehicle of change in your child's life." A proud adoptive foster parent raised her hand and said, "Don't you people understand that we are these children's first healthy teachers?" She was absolutely right. I had never heard a parent say that before and it was music to my ears. It confirmed that there are people out there in the world who understand the work to be done to move fostered or adopted children toward healthy self-esteem and success. These parents understand their importance and the role they hold in their fostered or adopted child's life. That understanding is what I have been talking about for years. It is what I have done in my work with these children and I have seen the positive results occur over and over again. If that amazing foster parent has seen that her "teachings" have made a difference in her adopted child's life, then it can make a difference for you as well.

I have written this book to help all parents, caregivers and professionals caring for fostered or adopted children and teens. This is a large population of children that many people do not understand. I did not when I began my work with foster children many years ago. I had to learn about these children and allow myself to go on a journey with them through their pain and healing.

This book is a guide for you to learn about how to build self-esteem within yourself and your fostered or adopted child or teen's life. It is based on my hands-on work with families and fostered and adopted children over the last 15 years. I will share with you my most effective tips and greatest accomplishments in building fostered and adopted children's self-esteem. When you complete this book, I hope you feel personally empowered to empower your fostered or adopted child or teen to move towards unlimited success.

I know from you, the foster parents, adoptive parents and professionals working with this population, how much you want to see these children become successful. I also know that, at times, the journey can be difficult, trying and frustrating. Being a biological parent, foster parent or adoptive parent includes good and difficult times. As a biological parent myself, I know this to be true.

If you can develop a strong belief within yourself that you possess the power to shape fostered and adopted children's lives, you can create success within your child. If you are not currently a foster or adoptive parent and want to become one, this book is also for you. If you are already a foster or adoptive parent, and have been struggling to find a way to break through to your fostered or adopted child, this book is for you too. I am a firm believer in second chances and believe that, given the right tools, change can occur at any time in one's life.

In this book, I will give you the tools to lead fostered and adopted children and teens towards leading a successful life. If you take these tools, and make them a part of your daily life, you will, I hope, lead your fostered or adopted child or teen towards achieving a successful life with confidence.

Fostered and adopted children and teens are filled with a great deal of fear in terms of their futures. They constantly worry about what will happen to them. They worry that no one will ever love or want to keep them. As you move through this book, please keep in mind that there are no perfect parents or children in this world. As professionals, working with these children, we also do not always know the exact steps to take to bring about success in fostered and adopted children and teens.

It has always been my belief that parents have to empower themselves emotionally first before they can help their child build their own healthy sense of self. Healthy self-esteem begins in the home. Likewise so can negative self-esteem. You may question this statement but every infant who comes into this world enters with high self-esteem. That self-esteem is then shaped first by the closest caregivers and then by the outside world. The good news is that if a child's self-esteem is shaped in a negative way from their first relationships, it can become positive with the right help and a "corrective emotional" experience.

The suggestions in this book are by no means a fool-proof cure for difficulties that you are experiencing with your fostered or adopted children or teens. They are, however, a guide that has been extremely successful for me in working with hundreds of fostered children, adopted children and professionals in the child welfare field. Although many of my thoughts focus on fostered children throughout the book, all the techniques can be applied to both fostered and adopted children and teens. I do hope that you can use many of the techniques in this book to help you form an unbreakable bond with your children. Remember however that what works for one person or child may not work for another. So, please try to use different techniques in this book to help you and your child or teen become successful. Take your time reading through the material, use what speaks to you the loudest and run with it!

My First Day on the Job

I knew nothing about foster children when I walked into a foster care and youth agency in Philadelphia, Pennsylvania. At the time, I had my Master's degree in counseling psychology and was working on obtaining my doctorate in clinical psychology. A friend at my wedding suggested I call the clinical director at the agency to schedule an interview to be an outpatient therapist with foster children. Two weeks later, I made the call to the director and began my journey of helping fostered and adopted children and parents find success.

During our interview, she informed me that working with foster children and their families can be very demanding and challenging. I learned later that she was not kidding. The work was both demanding and challenging but also exhilarating. She also informed me that working with the biological and foster parents can often be just as difficult and that many therapists do not last long in this field. With that great news I accepted the job! As I exited her office, she simply said, "Hope you are up for the challenge and I will see you on Monday."

The following Monday, I began my career as an outpatient therapist in foster care and I have not looked back since. It was 1999. On the drive into work, I kept thinking, "Is someone going to train me on how to work with these children?" What am I going to say to them? Good news, my boss did not throw me into the fire. For the first week, she gave me some books to read and I participated in some training. All the books that I was given talked about changing foster children's behaviors and creating a treatment plan that focused on changing behaviors. I'm a bit analytic and I kept asking myself, "But where are these behaviors coming from and why doesn't anyone care about this?" I learned early on in my schooling that behaviors derive from thoughts or actions. I also learned that in order to change a behavior, you must know where it is coming from or what is driving it to occur. I wanted to know what was causing this child to be disrespectful to their teacher. I wanted to know why the child was not following directions or was being disrespectful on a daily basis to their foster parents. There had to be a reason. As I began to work with the children, causes for their behavior were identified. Most of the causes centered on being raised by parents who abused them and did not acknowledge their existence.

I later learned that many of the other therapists were not making progress with their clients while I was. While they were focusing on changing behaviors, I was focused on changing lives. I met my first client on the third day of work. She was a ten-year-old African American young lady who had been in foster care for two years and was hoping to be adopted. The foster mother appeared to be invested in her life and treatment but like most foster parents could not understand why Tyla would not open up to her. Her chart read that she was abandoned by her mother who was using drugs and working as a prostitute. Tyla had two other siblings but did not know where they lived because the state separated them upon removal. Our first session went like this:

> She walked into my office with her head down. She was ten years old and had been placed into foster care. I introduced myself to her and she said, "Hello," in a very soft voice. I said that I was here to spend 50 minutes a week with her to get to know her. Following that exchange, she took her jacket off, lay down on my couch and put the jacket over her head. She said that she had nothing to say to me and that she had to be in therapy but no one said that she had to talk. This went on for one month. She would walk into my office, lie down on the couch and not talk to me. When the 50 minutes were up she rose from the couch and walked out. After the third time, I simply said, "I will be here for you when you are ready to talk." She did not respond, verbally that is. On the fifth visit, she emerged from her coat and said, "Do you

want to play cards?" "Yes," I replied and therapy began. For the next two years, we built a trustful relationship that began in silence.

I don't know what became of that beautiful child, as I had left that agency before she was placed for adoption. All I know is that from that first experience, I learned a very valuable lesson: trust is earned not given when it comes to connecting with an abused or neglected foster child.

In the late 1990s, I had the luxury of working with some foster children for two or three years. I had time to build trust slowly with the children. I had the time to get to know them, not only as a "damaged foster child," as many therapists called them, but as children who had dreams, goals and desires just like the children that were not in foster care. I never promised the child anything except for that during the time I was with them, I would be emotionally and physically present in their lives.

I have always believed that no one in the world has gone "untouched" by something traumatic in their life. The impact that trauma has on one's life is different for each child and adult. The truth is that we all have a chance to improve, grow and empower ourselves to overcome trauma.

CHAPTER 2

The Challenges of Parenting a Fostered or Adopted Child or Teen

Parenting any child has its challenges. If you choose to foster or adopt a child, you must believe that (1) you have the internal power and the skills to make positive change within the child's life and (2) you become the child's vehicle for change through your ability to show the child unconditional positive regard and acceptance despite what they have endured through abuse. In addition, you need to believe that you possess the ability to help this child build healthy self-esteem so that they have a second chance at a successful life. If you do not currently have this ability, the good news is that you can work on yourself to achieve it. When you have acheived this ability, and mastered your own self-worth, then I suggest you become a foster or adoptive parent.

I am fully aware that we do not live in a perfect world, nor are we perfect people. So, even with all of the self-empowerment work you have done on yourself, there will be days when that self-belief seems impossible. There will be days when you feel as though the life is being sucked out of you by your fostered or adopted children or teens. There will be days when you feel completely rejected and want to give up. These are the days when you must fight the most for these children because they are expecting you to give up on them, just as they may believe their biological parents gave up. Expect, however, that if you hang in there through the worst of times, accepting and guiding the child towards a safer, trusting world, where people do not leave but work toward making life better for them, you will see the best of times.

Fostered and adopted children and teens want to connect with you but they have not had the chance to develop the skills to do so. It has always been my belief that I needed to show these children how a healthy attachment forms between a caregiver and a child. I have always thought of myself as a therapist and a "vehicle" to teach fostered and adopted children the way to connect with people in a healthy manner. This is based on my belief that if we have positive healthy attachments and relationships with others, we feel good about ourselves and want to give the best part of ourselves to others.

Often, while providing daily therapy to fostered and adopted children, I was told by my supervisors, "You are too emotionally attached to these children." I would always say to myself, "No, you are not emotionally attached enough." For years, I thought to myself, "How do you not get emotionally attached to these innocent children?" I know as a therapist that we are taught to take our professional hats off when we leave the office. I was not able to accomplish that then or now, when it comes to helping fostered or adopted children. I am always thinking of ways to help move them and their families towards success. It doesn't interfere with my personal life. So what is the issue?

When I would think to myself about the clinical supervisors telling me to get my emotions in check, I would think, "Are you emotionally dead or are you protecting yourself from your own feelings of not being able to help the child you are working with?" That was the real question. Every day I met a new child or family, my first and only thought was "I can and will help you." It's worked this far for me. In most if not all treatment meetings I ever attended, many therapists cared more about getting their treatment plans approved and their behavioral goals correct than learning how to connect with foster children and build trust with them. I could never and still do not understand this mentality. I know that as professionals we all have protocol to follow, but I also think that learning about why your client needs to make progress is essential as well. Most of these children were presenting with low or no self-esteem. With this in mind, I kept asking myself, "Is focusing on changing their behavior the most essential aspect of these children's treatment?" Most of the children I counsel do not have a clue where their behaviors are coming from. I have made it my job to find out. After all, most if not all of the children placed into foster care come from abusive or neglected homes. It makes sense that they would have to build some trust with you before they trusted you to help them change their behavior. If I were abused, that is how I would want it to be. Wouldn't you? Think about it, would you just listen to a stranger tell you what to do or would you listen to a person who believes in you? I am sure your answer is that you would listen to the person who believes in you. It is no different for children. Why was I alone in my thinking? In my doctoral program we were taught that therapy is about the "relationship" you have with your clients. I can still hear my professor saying, "Don't you people understand that the relationship is the therapy?" It is still that way for me today in my private practice. I work towards building a relationship first with my clients. By taking this approach, progress occurs much more quickly and their self-esteem increases.

My doctorate professors taught us that therapy is about one thing: "the relationship." They would say, "If you can build a trusting relationship with your client then the rest of the treatment falls into place." I did not budge from my professors' beliefs when it came to working with fostered and adopted children and their families. While the other therapists were trying to get their fostered and adopted children to state three chores that they could help out with in their foster homes, I was asking the children to make three positive statements about themselves. We were building a trustful relationship. The reason that most fostered or adopted children are placed into the foster care system is because of abuse, neglect and an unhealthy relationship with their biological family members. I believe that the only way to change how fostered or adopted children or teens relate to others is to give them a "corrective emotional" experience. Through the use of myself, I show them how to create a meaningful, trusting, accountable relationship. I teach the children and teens that there are people out in the world that can care for you and that you can trust. This concept will be explored in more detail later in the book.

I was making wonderful progress with the children and parents I was helping. We were connecting, sharing feelings and slowly moving towards building self-esteem both in the parents and in the children. My clients did not miss their appointments. They were eager to come. I wanted the children, teens and parents to see that:

1. I believed in them

2. they were worthy

3. they were important to me and themselves

4. they deserved happiness.

With these four approaches to treatment trust began to form and progress began to take place. While the other therapists were showing up to team meetings sharing their frustrations that the kids on their caseloads could not change their behaviors, I was sharing my progress.

Look, I'm not saying that trying to help fostered or adopted children's behaviors is not an important part of treatment. It is but it is *not* where you should begin treatment or begin bonding with your fostered or adopted child. Parents and professionals need to be aware that fostered or adopted children's concept of trust and dependency have been shattered. They are afraid of attaching to other adults in fear of continued abandonment. They push love away because they feel they don't deserve it. They are engaging in destructive behaviors because they are wondering, "How are you any different from the other adults who have hurt me before?"

They are also wondering, "How can I trust you? You resemble the adults that hurt me. How are you different?" Foster and adoptive parents, the best advice I can give to you is that you must *prove* to these untrusting children and teens that you are different from their former caregivers. It is not the child's responsibility to prove to you that they can follow your rules, have perfect behaviors and be a child who pleases. If you are thinking in this way, then you have *not* prepared yourself properly for this journey of healing and connecting with your fostered or adopted child.

The "proving" process will not happen right away. So don't expect that to occur. The process can move along more quickly if you begin your bonding experience by accepting where the fostered or adopted child or teen is emotionally and move them towards healthy bonding with you by creating that trusting relationship. The fostered or adopted child or teen's self-esteem flourishes from the relationship.

CHAPTER 3

Attachment and Self-Esteem

Two Critical Aspects of Connecting with a Fostered or Adopted Child or Teen

"Creating self-esteem within any child begins with building a trustful relationship."

In psychology, the term "self-esteem" is used to describe a person's overall sense of self-worth or personal value. Self-esteem is often seen as a personality trait, which means that it tends to be stable and enduring. Self-esteem can involve a variety of beliefs about the self, such as the appraisal of one's own appearance, beliefs, emotions and behaviors (New, 2012).

Healthy self-esteem is like a child's armor against the challenges of the world. Kids who know their strengths and weaknesses and feel good about themselves seem to have an easier time handling conflicts and resisting negative pressures. They tend to smile more readily and enjoy life. These kids are realistic and generally optimistic. In contrast, kids with low self-esteem can find challenges to be sources of major anxiety and frustration. Those who think poorly of themselves have a hard time finding solutions to problems. If the child gives in to self-critical thoughts such as "I'm no good" or "I can't do anything right," they may become passive, withdrawn or depressed.

Faced with a new challenge, their immediate response might be "I can't" (New, 2012).

Patterns of self-esteem start very early in life. The concept of success following effort and persistence starts early. Once people reach adulthood, it's harder to make changes to how they see and define themselves (New, 2012). Research shows that when parents are involved with their children the children have higher grades and test scores, decreased use of drugs and alcohol, fewer instances of violent behavior, increased motivation and better self-esteem (Chen and Fan, 2001). Parents and caregivers can promote healthy self-esteem by showing encouragement and enjoyment in spending time with the child in many areas of a child's life (New, 2012; Ryan, Stiller and Lynch, 1994).

Throughout my years of intense schooling, I learned about one very important aspect to creating self-esteem in anyone: it's about building a healthy relationship with another person who accepts you unconditionally. I know you may be saying, "Does that ever really happen?" The answer is yes. In fact, people in these relationships are the individuals who tend to have the highest self-esteem. Think about this for a minute or two. Are you most happy when your relationships are in harmony or discord? I'm sure you answered, "Harmony." Toxic relationships suck the life out of people and deplete their energy. They are unhealthy for adults and children. These types of relationships often help us to question our own self-worth and make us feel irritable and sad most of the time. On the other hand, people report that healthy relationships make them feel respected and content (Johnson, 2011).

If you look up parenting and self-esteem on the internet you will see article after article about how parents have the most influence on a child's self-esteem. This is for a reason. It is because it is true. Children develop their first sense of self within their relationship with their caregivers. If the child is provided with unconditional love, security, protection and acknowledgement on a consistent basis then it is likely that they will feel good about themselves. If they are provided with deprivation, criticism and rejection they are likely to have low self-worth (Bowlby, 1973).

The majority of the children who are being adopted from foster care unfortunately fall into the low self-worth category due to parental abusive and/or neglectful treatment prior to placement. I believe that children are brought into the world with a blank slate otherwise known as a tabula rasa. This means that every child has a chance to develop high self-esteem. After all, children are not born feeling good or bad about themselves. That develops through their influences and interactions within their environment.

Environmental influences, such as family and peer interaction, have a major effect on a child's early development. In my earlier research on ambiguous loss[1] within foster children (Schecter-Cornbluth, 2006) I studied the effect of early family influence on foster children/teens' development. I found that there are specific characteristics of parents that help foster positive and negative self-esteem in children.

Parents who are attentive to their child's needs and are available on a consistent basis from infancy have the best chance of raising a child with high self-esteem. Children who are raised by parents who are inattentive, emotionally absent, inconsistent and unavailable have a strong chance of developing low self-esteem (Schecter-Cornbluth, 2006).

---

1   Ambiguous loss is a term used to describe the grief distress associated with an unresolved loss. I found in my own research that fostered and adopted children keep their birth parents psychologically alive even though they are not physically present.

Here are the top four parental characteristics.

Parental Characteristics that promote Positive Self-Esteem in Children	Parental Characteristics that promote Negative Self-Esteem in Children
1. Attentiveness 2. Being emotionally present 3. Consistency 4. Availability	1. Inattentiveness 2. Being emotionally absent 3. Inconsistency 4. Unavailability

Formation of Self-Esteem

Dr. Sears (2011), the guru of early parenting information in my opinion, claims that self-esteem is your child's passport to lifelong mental health and social happiness. Sears claims that it is the foundation of a child's well-being and the key to success as an adult. At all ages, how you feel about yourself affects how you act. Think about a time when you were feeling really good about yourself. You probably found it much easier to get along with others and feel good about them.

Dr. Sears is completely correct. When people feel good about themselves, they are able to accomplish more and get along better with others. Self-image is also a big part of self-esteem. When children feel that they are able to accomplish something and are supported, they feel better about themselves.

Self-Image

The child looks in the mirror and likes the person they see. They look inside themselves and are comfortable with the person they see. They must think of this self as being someone who can make things happen and who is worthy of love. How people value themselves, get along with others, perform at school, achieve at work, and relate in marriage, all stems from the strength of their self-image (Sears, 2011).

Parents are the main source of a child's sense of self-esteem. Healthy attachment is the key to a child's self-esteem. If young children learn at a very young age what consistent and responsive caregiving is and continue to receive it throughout their lives, they are likely to be content (Sears, 2011).

Let's begin our journey towards self-esteem by learning about building healthy attachments between a fostered or adopted child and an adult. This is a critical aspect to developing confidence in these children.

Healthy Attachment

Early healthy attachment between a parent and a child is the ultimate key to a child's future success. Even if trauma occurs to a child after a healthy attachment has been formed, the initial healthy bond makes it much easier for the child to recover.

So how does a healthy relationship form between a caregiver and a child? Well, it begins with what is known as an "attachment dance." Think about this for a minute; when a baby is born, they need to have their needs met on a consistent basis to feel safe and secure. What I mean by this is that they need to be fed and have their diaper changed when they cry. They need to be held when they feel panic or fear. When a parent does this on a consistent basis, the child forms a healthy secure attachment to the parent. The child feels loved and acknowledged.

This early healthy attachment bond is in my belief the most critical aspect to a child's future relations with others. I am not alone in my thinking. A landmark report, published in 2000 by the Committee on Integrating the Science of Early Childhood Development, identified how crucial the attachment bond is to a child's development. This form of communication affects the way your child develops mentally, physically, intellectually, emotionally and socially. While attachment occurs naturally as you, the parent or caretaker, care for your baby's needs, the quality of the attachment bond varies.

- A *secure* attachment bond ensures that your child will feel secure and understood, and be calm enough to experience optimal development of their nervous system. Your child's developing brain organizes itself to provide your child with the best foundation for life: a feeling of safety that results in eagerness to learn, healthy self-awareness, trust and empathy.

- An *insecure* attachment bond fails to meet your child's need for security, understanding and calm, preventing the child's developing brain from organizing itself in the best ways. This can inhibit emotional, mental and even physical development, leading to difficulties in learning and forming relationships in later life.

Developing a secure attachment bond between you and your child, and giving your child the best start in life, does not require you to be a perfect parent. In fact, the 2000 study found that the critical aspect of the child–primary caretaker relationship is *not* based on quality of care, educational input, or even the bond of love that develops between parent and infant. Rather, it is based on the quality of the nonverbal communication process that takes place between you and your child.

I completely agree with this study, especially on the concept of being a "perfect" parent. There are no perfect parents or children. However, there is something known as good enough parenting. What I mean by this is that, as parents, we cannot always give the best of ourselves every minute of every day to our children. What we can do is give enough of ourselves to be consistent. If we are tired and don't want to go and answer our child's screams, we still do it because we know that our child's needs are more important than our own.

Your dedication to your child's needs is what provides them with the early building blocks for healthy attachment. The fact is that, as parents, we have been given an incredible amount of power to shape our child's development. What matters the most is that you use your power to encourage growth.

Children who are provided with a healthy attachment early on learn several important attachment skills. Here is a short list of some of these skills:

- learn basic trust and reciprocity, which serves as a template for all future emotional relationships

- explore the environment with feelings of safety and security ("secure base" (Bowlby, 1990)), which leads to healthy cognitive and social development

- develop the ability to self-regulate, which results in effective management of impulses and emotions

- create a foundation for the formation of identity, which includes a sense of competency, self-worth, and a balance between dependence and autonomy

- establish a prosocial moral framework, which involves empathy, compassion and conscience

- generate the core belief system, which comprises cognitive appraisals of self, caregivers, others and life in general

- provide a defense against stress and trauma, which incorporates resourcefulness and resiliency.

(Levy and Orlans, 2014)

Children who begin their lives with the essential foundation of secure attachment fare better in all aspects of functioning as development unfolds. Numerous longitudinal studies have demonstrated that securely attached infants and toddlers do better over time in the following areas:

- self-esteem

- independence and autonomy

- resiliency in the face of adversity

- ability to manage impulses and feelings

- long-term friendships

- relationships with parents, caregivers and other authority figures

- prosocial coping skills

- trust, intimacy and affection

- positive and hopeful belief systems about self, family and society

- empathy, compassion and conscience

- behavioral performance and academic success in school

- promoting secure attachment in their own children when they become adults.

(Srofe *et al.*, 2005)

The core beliefs of children who have experienced secure attachments in the early years are as follows:

- *Self:* "I am good, wanted, worthwhile, competent and lovable."

- *Caregivers:* "They are appropriately responsive to my needs, sensitive, dependable, caring and trustworthy."

- *Life:* "My world feels safe; life is worth living."

(Levy and Orlans, 2014)

Why am I explaining all of this to you? I want you to know that it is critical to understand that if an infant is cared for consistently, but not necessarily perfectly, they know what to expect and it helps with self-regulation and self-esteem. We call this "attachment parenting" in psychology. In real life, we call this "guiding our child to move towards high self-esteem." Now, I know as a mother myself, that there will be days when you are on edge or don't respond to your child's cries as quickly as you could. That is perfectly okay. The point here is that if parents respond to their children on a consistent basis, the child learns what to expect and self-regulation occurs.

If children are not invited to the attachment dance early on in their development, then they often remain in the corner. This is the pattern of many fostered or adopted children who are placed into the foster care system or adopted after the early stages of development. These children, overall, do not receive consistent care. They often do not know what that looks or feels like. Therefore, when you provide consistency for them, they reject your overtures. Fostered and adopted children have to relearn or learn for the first time what consistent caregiving is. Give these children a chance to accomplish this important goal.

When one feels trapped, helpless and rejected, it is impossible to feel good about yourself. The same goes for children. Children who are placed into foster care or adopted were probably not provided with an attachment dance. They also were not provided with consistent care. This often leads fostered and adopted children to feel rejected and helpless.

Insecure Attachments

We have discussed secure attachments. Now it is even more critical that you understand how an insecure attachment bond affects a child's development. This section will help you understand why fostered or adopted children and teens may have such a difficult time bonding with foster and adoptive parents.

What one is not given emotionally or physically early on in life can affect one's later development. Insecure attachment early on between a child and a parent is a catalyst to later emotional difficulties and low self-esteem in children. The good news is that it can be corrected.

Insecure attachment is formed when a caregiver and their infant do not do a healthy "attachment dance." Instead, it is a "dysfunctional dance" where the infant does not get their needs met on a consistent basis. When this occurs, the child fails to thrive emotionally, cognitively and physically. Let's look at the following scenario to gain a better understanding of how this works.

Timmy was born to his mother Veronica, who was not married and had been living at or below the poverty line for the last ten years. She was a victim of physical and sexual abuse as a young child. When Timmy was born, she was very stressed and did not have much support or guidance to raise Timmy. There were days when Timmy would be left in a soiled diaper for hours. He was fed when Veronica had food or when she did not sleep through the feeding times. Timmy would cry for her constantly but she would scream, "Shut up" and slam the door. Eventually social services were called and Timmy was placed into the foster care system.

This scenario is an example of how an insecure or dysfunctional attachment forms between a parent and their infant. The infant is not receiving what they need from the parent to thrive. Instead they are receiving reactions that often cause them to avoid attaching to one another.

Research has shown that up to 80 percent of high-risk families (where there is abuse and neglect, poverty, substance abuse, domestic violence, history of maltreatment in parents' childhood, depression or other psychological disorders in parents) create severe attachment disorders in their children (Levy and Orlans, 2014).

Disrupted and anxious attachment not only leads to emotional and social problems, but also results in biochemical consequences in the developing brain. Infants raised without loving touch and security have abnormally high levels of stress hormones, which can impair the growth and development of their brains and bodies. The neurobiological consequences of emotional neglect can leave children behaviorally disordered, depressed, apathetic, slow to learn and prone to chronic illness. Compared to securely attached children, attachment disordered children are significantly more likely to be aggressive, disruptive and antisocial. Disruption of attachment during the crucial first three years of life can lead to what has been called "affectionless psychopathy," the inability to form meaningful emotional relationships, coupled with chronic anger, poor impulse control and a lack of remorse (Levy and Orlans, 2014).

Children lacking secure attachments with caregivers are at high risk of growing up to be parents who are incapable of establishing this crucial foundation with their own children. Instead of following the instinct to protect, nurture and love their children, they abuse, neglect and abandon (Levy and Orlans, 2014).

Children who begin their lives with compromised and disrupted attachment are at risk of the following serious problems as development unfolds:

- low self-esteem

- needy or clingy behaviors

- withdrawing when faced with stress and adversity

- lack of self-control

- inability to develop and maintain friendships

- being alienated from and oppositional with parents, caregivers and other authority figures

- antisocial attitudes and behaviors

- aggression and violence

- difficulty with genuine trust, intimacy and affection

- having a negative, hopeless and pessimistic view of self, family and society

- lacking empathy, compassion and remorse

- behavioral and academic problems at school

- perpetuating the cycle of maltreatment and attachment disorder in their own children when they reach adulthood.

(Levy and Orlans, 2014)

Children who experience this kind of insecure attachment often develop care beliefs as follows:

- *Self:* "I am bad, unwanted, worthless, helpless and unlovable."

- *Caregivers:* "They are unresponsive to my needs, insensitive, hurtful and untrustworthy."

- *Life:* "My world feels unsafe; life is painful and burdensome."

(Levy and Orlans, 2014)

Fostered and adopted children and teens who have experienced insecure and/or dysfunctional attachments are often susceptible to serious emotional developmental issues as children and adults. The good news is that they can become survivors of this kind of attachment with the help of new caregivers.

Self-Esteem in the Traumatized Child

Early childhood trauma can lead to low self-esteem in children. Trauma is defined as a psychologically distressing event that is outside the range of usual human experience, one that induces an abnormally intense and prolonged stress response (Mueser *et al.*, 2002).

Children and adolescents experience trauma under two different sets of circumstances. Some types of traumatic events involve (1) experiencing a serious injury to yourself or witnessing a serious injury to, or the death of, someone else, (2) facing imminent threats of serious injury or death to yourself or others, or (3) experiencing a violation of personal physical integrity. These experiences usually call forth overwhelming feelings of terror, horror or helplessness. Because these events occur at a particular time and place and are usually short-lived, we refer to them as *acute traumatic events*. These kinds of traumatic events include the following (Mueser *et al.*, 2002):

- school shootings

- gang-related violence in the community

- terrorist attacks

- natural disasters (for example, earthquakes, floods or hurricanes)

- serious accidents (for example, car or motorcycle crashes)

- sudden or violent loss of a loved one

- physical or sexual assault (for example, being beaten, shot or raped).

In other cases, according to Mueser, exposure to trauma can occur repeatedly over long periods of time. These experiences call forth a range of responses, including intense feelings of fear, loss of trust in others, decreased sense of personal safety, guilt and shame. We call these kinds of trauma *chronic traumatic situations*. These kinds of traumatic situations include the following:

- some forms of physical abuse

- long-standing sexual abuse

- domestic violence

- neglect.

Child traumatic stress occurs when children and adolescents are exposed to traumatic events or traumatic situations, and when this exposure overwhelms their ability to cope with what they have experienced.

Depending on their age, children respond to traumatic stress in different ways. Many children show signs of intense distress such as disturbed sleep, difficulty paying attention and concentrating, anger and irritability, withdrawal, repeated and intrusive thoughts, and show extreme distress when confronted by anything that reminds them of their traumatic experiences. Some children develop psychiatric conditions such as posttraumatic stress disorder, depression, anxiety and a variety of behavioral disorders.

While some children "bounce back" after adversity, traumatic experiences can result in a significant disruption of child or adolescent development and have profound long-term consequences. Repeated exposure to traumatic events can affect the child's brain and nervous system and increase the risk of low academic performance, engagement in high-risk behaviors, and difficulties in peer and family relationships. Traumatic stress can cause increased use of health and mental health services and increased involvement with the child welfare and juvenile justice systems. Adult survivors of traumatic events may have difficulty in establishing fulfilling relationships, holding steady jobs and becoming productive members of our society. Fortunately, there are effective treatments for child traumatic stress (National Child Traumatic Stress Network, 2013).

In my opinion and through my experience, most fostered and adopted children and teens are traumatized children (Bass, Shields and Behrman, 2004). The majority of these children are either witnesses to violence or victims of personal violations. The trauma that many foster children experience prior to coming into care causes them to have low self-worth. Most of the behavioral problems that professionals and foster and adoptive parents see from the children are due to the child's feelings of low self-worth and the lack of opportunities afforded to them to gain that self-worth early on in development.

People ask me all the time, "How do you raise a fostered or adopted child's self-esteem when they have been abused, abandoned, put down and rejected?" My answer is always the same, "Very slowly, with a great deal of patience, hard work and education." A fostered or adopted child's self-esteem will increase based on your positive, encouraging reaction and behaviors towards them. Many fostered or adopted children have experienced some kind of trauma before being placed into your home. All of the children I worked with entered my office with some form of trauma. When a child experiences a trauma, many aspects of who they once were or could have been changes. For example, if the child was once outgoing, they can become withdrawn. A child who was outspoken can become silent. A child who was trustful becomes mistrustful.

Trauma affects how one views oneself and others. The act of trauma shakes a child's foundation and inner core. It also affects the people in the child's world. The positive side to this, if there is one, is that many children have much more resiliency (inner strength to overcome trauma) in recovering from trauma than adults. This means that if the child receives help immediately following the trauma they have a good chance of recovering from the traumatic event. The longer a child goes without therapeutic treatment following a trauma, the longer they will take to recover.

Children who experience trauma such as neglect or physical, sexual or emotional abuse will often show the following behaviors or symptoms. I am sure you have seen some of these symptoms in your own children you care for:

- trouble sleeping or falling asleep

- nightmares or unwanted memories of the event

- problems concentrating or paying attention

- difficulty getting along with family or friends or becoming less social

- increase or decrease in appetite

- behaviors more appropriate to a younger child such as bed-wetting, clinging to caregivers or thumb-sucking

- anger and other emotional outbursts

- avoidance of people, places and things that remind them of the event

- nervousness or startling easily

- depression

- increased problems with school and grades.

(National Child Traumatic Stress Network, 2013)

Trauma may appear as the following:

Table 3.1 Symptoms of Trauma

Preschool: age five and younger	• Preschoolers may re-enact the traumatic event through their play. • Their minds might be stuck on a specific part of the event. • They may become more clingy than before the traumatic incident. • They may become passive and quiet. • They may avoid new people or situations because of fears related to the trauma. • They may become easily alarmed and generally more fearful of being away from caregivers. • They are strongly affected by parental reactions. • Preschoolers may also have problems with feeding or toileting when they have not typically had these problems in the past.
School age: 6 to 11	• School-age children may draw pictures of the traumatic event. • They may also go back and forth between being shy and withdrawn or being unusually aggressive. • They may have sleep problems (restless sleep, talking in sleep, waking up tired). • They may have problems concentrating in school. • They may complain of stomach aches or headaches. • School-age children may also respond to very general reminders of the event, such as a particular color, smell or sound.

Adolescents: age 12 to 18	• Adolescents may fear that their "flashbacks" mean that they are sick or crazy. • They are likely to avoid thoughts or feelings related to the event. • Some will try to avoid memories of the event by using drugs or alcohol. • They are likely to be more irritable than usual. • They might seem as if they have a lot of problems paying attention in school when they have no previous history of attention problems. • Adolescents may also have sleep problems that are disguised as late night studying, television-watching or partying.

Source: adapted from Levy and Orlans, 1998

People often ask me if developmental age has an effect on how you increase a child's self-esteem. My response to this question is "Yes and no." My technique of building self-esteem is working on building a trusting relationship with the child or teenager. I certainly can't talk to a five-year-old as I would to a 16-year-old. However, I can focus on building trust with a child at any age. Trust is the key component to helping fostered and adopted children and adolescents move towards feeling more positive about themselves. You see, if kids trust you enough, they will begin to feel comfortable enough to share their feelings with you. By sharing their feelings with you they feel acknowledged and that leads to self-confidence.

Here are two examples of how I would begin building self-esteem in a fostered or adopted child at the age of eight years old and 16 years old.

Michael, Eight Years Old, Placed into Foster Care Due to Neglect by Biological Mother

DR. SUE: Hi, Michael. Last time we met, we talked a little bit about how everyone is different from each other. Remember I told you that I am short and other people are tall. You told me in session that you are different because you don't live with your "real parents." I was wondering if you could tell me how that makes you feel about yourself?

MICHAEL: Not so good, I guess. I wish I could be like everyone else.

DR. SUE: You know, Michael, no one is like everyone else. We are all different and go through different things in life. But what you are saying about being different, I get it. I think I would feel the same way as you do if I did not live with my real parents. I might even think that I was different too and that does not feel good. (*Here I am joining with Michael and how he is thinking.*)

MICHAEL: Yeah really, you would feel that way?

DR. SUE: Sure I would. I would not be happy about it. It does not seem fair to me.

MICHAEL: Thanks, Dr. Sue, you are cool.

Tina, Age 17, Placed into Foster Care at Nine Years Old, Adopted at 11 Years Old

DR. SUE: Hi, Tina. Remember in our last session, we talked about your feelings about doubting your abilities to go to college? Let's look at that again, okay?

TINA: Sure, but I already told you, I want to go to college but everyone in my family says I'm just going to end up like my crack head mother. *(Tina still has contact with her birth parents.)*

DR. SUE: Do you believe what others are telling you, Tina? Let's look at the evidence together, okay?

TINA: Okay, I guess.

DR. SUE: Well, first, do you smoke crack? Second, did your mother graduate high school? Third, are you a good student? Fourth, are you the same person as your mother? Fifth, do you have your adopted parents and my support backing you?

TINA: Wow! I never thought of it like that. I never realized that I was so different from my mom until we looked at it that way.

These are two real life examples of children to whom I provided therapy. In the first example, Michael is struggling with feeling different from the other children because he is in foster care. This is a very common issue for children in placement. After all, due to their circumstances they are different from other children who live with their biological families. The goal in my approach to Michael is simply to join with him where he is in his thinking. By doing this I acknowledge that he may feel different and that it is okay. When one feels validated, one feels accepted and self-acceptance is a key to healthy self-esteem.

In my second example with Tina, she is doubting her abilities based on false information she is telling herself. Teenagers often walk around with what is known as a fable or a make-believe story of what they think is the reality of themselves. The truth is that the fable is usually incorrect. Teenagers need evidence to change their minds about their thoughts. I gave Tina the evidence she needed to counteract her negative false thoughts about herself. What I was teaching Tina was "self-reliance." This is another crucial aspect of building high self-esteem because it teaches a teen to reduce their reliance on other people's opinions and evaluations. I also showed Tina that she has support from other people to guide her and help her reach her goal. All of these factors led Tina to see her own truth.

Were Michael and Tina able to come to these realizations overnight? Of course not and don't fool yourself into thinking you can just apply these techniques a couple of times and automatically your fostered or adopted child will have high self-esteem. That would be foolish. Instead, remember that it takes dedication and repetition of these approaches to see change. With consistency, a fostered or adopted child with low self-esteem can move towards high self-esteem.

Deborah Plummer (2007) in her book *Helping Children to Build Self-Esteem* offers an excellent summary on how to build self-esteem for a child who has faced many life challenges. Plummer states that, "In more extreme cases, the psychological effects of neglect or lack of loving relationships during babyhood will certainly severely complicate the recovery pattern. The task of helping such troubled children to regain self-esteem or to build self-esteem where none exists is therefore very complex" (p.26). Plummer goes on to say that, at the same time, we should not underestimate the impact on a child's life of a caring adult who is able to "be there" for them and to hear their story with acceptance, empathy and wisdom.

Plummer believes, as do I, that as parents or caregivers, we can support children with limited self-esteem by:

1. being curious about their internal monologue (meaning their theory about who they are)

2. showing them unconditional genuine warmth and respect for their individuality

3. being aware of how our actions and words affect their self-concept

4. helping them to make realistic self-evaluations

5. helping them to understand that self-esteem goes up and down and that this is "normal"

6. helping them to see that they are worthy, important and special in their own way

7. allowing them to understand that everyone makes mistakes and helping them to learn from these mistakes

8. teaching them self-determination

9. teaching them self-acceptance and that no one in life has a perfect slate. Tragedy can happen to everyone. It's what you do with it that matters

10. showing them that one can move from being a victim to being a survivor

11. teaching them about forgiveness and self-love.

(Plummer, 2007; Schecter-Cornbluth, 2006)

Remember that you are the force to create change in a fostered or adopted child's life. These children are looking to you to teach them how to form attachments and feel worthy. The way that I have always begun this process with fostered or adopted children is through giving them what I mentioned early on in the book, a "corrective emotional experience."

CHAPTER 4

Providing a Child or Teen with a "Corrective Emotional Experience"

Corrective Emotional Experience

The majority of foster children are placed into the system due to some kind of abuse. In my experience, the issue these children struggle with the most is establishing and rebuilding trust with new adults. Who can blame them after what some of these children have experienced?

Think about it for yourself for a minute. You are eight years old, and you rely on your parents to take care of you. They are emotionally present and physically present to meet your needs, thus you are for the most part a well-adjusted kid. Well, that is how every child wants their life to be. Now imagine a different scenario: you live with your mother who is physically present but emotionally absent. She is hardly ever home and when she is she is drinking and ignoring you. You still love her because she is your mother but you do not trust that she can take care of you. One day, you return home from school and your mother is gone. You are taken to a strange place to live with strange people who you do not know. At least with your mother, you knew what to expect even though it was abusive.

All of a sudden you are placed with strangers, who are foreign to you. They do not look like your family and certainly do not resemble anything that reminds you of your life. You feel scared, afraid and depressed about what is happening to you. It is just so confusing. However, you are in this place and you need someone to help you understand what is happening and what your future holds. You need someone to tell you the truth. You need someone to comfort you or at least try even though you may push that comfort away. You need a new healthy teacher for a while (or forever, depending on if you become adopted) to help guide you in coming to some sort of terms with the fact that this is your life for a while. Who is that person? It's *you*, their foster or adopted parent or professional providing their therapeutic treatment.

I approach every fostered or adopted child or teen who walks into my office with the same thinking. I want to be their "corrective emotional experience." I see myself as the person or the force that can help each and every child overcome the trauma they have suffered and propel them to a place that they never imagined they could reach—a successful life. After reading about my process of providing a corrective emotional experience, I hope you will be able to do the same for the kids you care for. As I have mentioned before, you have been given an amazing gift to help heal a child's life and help them to develop into a productive individual and give them the life that they deserve. If you see your role as such, then you will also develop a wonderful close relationship with this child. If you let your frustration get in the way of this process, then you will have extreme difficulty bonding with a foster child. I can guarantee this every time. I'm not saying that there will not be times when you become frustrated; we all do, as parents of fostered, adopted and biological children. However, with fostered or adopted children, you have the added job (yes, job) of helping the child sort through the trauma and the lack of trust they have for adults. In order to do this, you have to check your own self-esteem. Then you have to put this child before yourself and your own needs for a while. You have to be prepared for a long journey of ups and downs. As I said, it begins with you seeing yourself as a "corrective vehicle of change" in the child's life. Let's dive into this now.

A "corrective emotional experience" can simply be defined as teaching an individual healthy ways to express their emotions or behaviors. This is accomplished through modeling appropriate healthy attachment behaviors. Many fostered and adopted children come from abusive or neglectful homes where they did not experience a healthy emotional connection. As has been discussed, this will have caused them to have low self-esteem. Most likely, they did not have much structure in their home nor do they know how to show respect to others because none was shown to them. So, they need to relearn how to do this through your example as their role model.

You can teach fostered and adopted children to respect themselves and you through being consistent with the child and beginning your healthy bonding process with these tips. A corrective emotional experience begins with:

1. Showing the Child or Teen You Believe in Them So You Can Form Trust

Early on in treatment with a foster child, my only goal is to form a trusting relationship with the child. I do not focus on the trauma right away. All that does is scare them off and allows them to think that it is the only thing I "want" from them. No one, even a child, wants to talk about something that causes them shame. It is embarrassing to talk about abuse. Instead, I get to know the child's likes and dislikes. I ask them questions about who they are and what they like to do. I get to know them as a child beyond their title of foster child. After all, we all have other names, don't we? I am also a mother, wife, professor and a therapist. But first I am Sue and I am not going to let anyone into my world and share my most intimate secrets and details of my personal life without some serious trust. Would you?

2. Letting the Child or Teen Know They Are Worthy

We all want to feel that we matter to people, especially to the people who brought us into the world. Foster children do not feel this for the most part. Instead, they feel rejected, unworthy, abandoned and alone. I found that, as a therapist working these children, it was critically important to let them know from the beginning that what happened to them was not their fault and that they deserved a better life than was provided for them. I simply say:

> "I am sorry for what has happened to you. You deserved to grow up in a home that was able to provide you with everything you needed, such as a parent who was there for you all the time, food, water, etc. I know that I may not be able to understand everything that you went through but for the time I am here with you, I will be here with you. I will listen to you. I will comfort you and I will acknowledge you because that is what you deserve."

In my 16 years of doing this work with fostered and adopted children and teens, that approach has never failed. I may have to do it a hundred times but I always get a great response back in the end. I get the response of trust.

3. Letting the Child or Teen Know They Have Value

We all want to feel valued and told that we are "good." Many fostered and adopted children grew up in an environment where their own parents did not value themselves, therefore they were not taught how to build value within themselves. Therefore as their "corrective teacher" I see that as one of my jobs. This can be accomplished by finding out what they have talents for and honing in on them. For example, a wonderful therapist told me once that she had a child who loved fishing. It was the only thing that he spoke about. So she took it upon herself to bring into her session with the child as many fishing magazines as she could find. This showed the child that what he was saying had value to her. His wishes were acknowledged and he internalized that as his voice having value. In this field of work or caregiving, we always have to go the extra mile for these kids. We must show them that they have value. We must teach them that their value is in their voice or their dreams and it must be recognized and honored by you.

Notice that I did not say "letting them know they are loved." Don't get me wrong, I do believe that love is extremely important in helping a fostered or adopted child grow and you certainly should give that to them as well. However, every tip I just suggested to you builds that love and trust. Love is a wonderful thing, as they say, but it is not everything in any relationship. Oh, and by the way, it may be that the foster child's birth parents loved them very much but look what happened in that circumstance. Love is important but it is not enough in healing a child from trauma, nor is it the only emotion that helps a child build self-esteem.

4. Letting the Child or Teen Know They Are Important

Who does not want to feel important? I do. I have looked up a great deal of definitions over the years of what the term "important" actually means and my favorite one from the dictionary is "mattering." I like this particular definition because all children need to "matter" to their parents and others in their life to feel good about themselves. Every child needs to be recognized as being significant in order to feel important and have self-confidence. Fostered and adopted children appear not to always "matter" to their biological parents. Sometimes, their biological parents are physically but not emotionally present. Emotional presence is what shows children that they "matter." Importance is derived from a parent praising a child for accomplishments and helping them to understand when they do something wrong. Yes, disciplining a child (in a nonviolent way) and setting boundaries shows a child they matter too. Many foster children never received either, so they do not even know if they are important. It is therefore your job as their healthy teacher to show them that they "matter" so they can identify themselves as being important.

The best way I know how to show the child or teen they are important is by simply telling them they are special and unique to you. Having the child accept these words of praise is challenging and takes time and consistency.

I specifically remember one 11-year-old foster child who said to me, "How can I ever think that I am important if my own mother just threw me away like trash?" My answer was, "Are you going to let one person define who you are?" Her answer: "No. I guess not. I never thought about it like that."

It really does not take much to help a child feel important. It does, however, take a conscious effort on your part to be emotionally present in their lives and take an interest in who they are as a person. That means not looking at them always as a fostered or adopted child but just looking at them as a child who needs acknowledgement to grow, just as a plant needs water to grow. If you can add the water, meaning the acknowledgment, I think you will be amazed how the child can grow and build self-worth.

5. Letting the Child or Teen Know They Deserve Happiness

A great number of foster children I have counseled did not believe that they would ever have happiness in their lives. Some of the children believed they did not deserve to be happy. The abuse that they had suffered made them feel unworthy of happiness. They felt bad about themselves and believed all they deserved in life was more disappointment. Who could blame them, considering what many of them had suffered from the people who were supposed to love them the most and provide them with opportunities for happiness, their parents. This was the part of therapy that really made me feel so sad. To watch and listen to a young child who has their whole life in front of them say, "I don't deserve to be happy" is devastating. It was at these times I wanted to cry for their pain. The sadness for me was because they did nothing wrong to deserve the unhappiness they felt inside. They did nothing to cause the neglect or abuse their parents caused. These children are victims of circumstances beyond their control. Yet so many kids say, "If I just was better, my mother or father would not have had to hurt me." This is when you intervene with the "It's not your fault" comments.

Do you know what makes people happiest? No, it's not money. It's quality relationships. It's knowing that you can rely on someone to be there to comfort you when you are in pain. It is also knowing that you have a caring person in your life who is reliable.

Most people do not realize that they are in control of their happiness. The one thing that blocks our happiness more than anything else is the belief that we won't achieve complete happiness because we don't really deserve to be happy. If a child has consistently been telling themselves that they do not deserve happiness, then how on earth will they find a desire to be happy? Here is the clue: you need to help them understand that they deserve happiness. You begin this by helping them to silence the voice in their head telling them to be unhappy. You introduce simple things into their lives such as spending time with them to introduce the concept of happiness. You can also help them to change their irrational beliefs about themselves by suggesting that each time they think something negative about themselves they could replace it with a positive thought. I was successful in accomplishing this with a 15-year-old adopted child who would always say to herself, "I will never have friends." We changed her negative thought to "Maybe I will make a new friend today."

A Corrective Emotional Experience and Unconditional Positive Regard for a Fostered or Adopted Child

All of the techniques described above can be consolidated into one term which is "unconditional positive regard." This is your number one tool for ongoing success with fostered and adopted children. It is also your ticket to helping them to build healthy self-esteem.

Unconditional positive regard, a term popularly believed to have been coined by the humanistic psychologist Carl Rogers (1961), is, by his definition, basic acceptance and support of a person regardless of what the person says or does. Rogers believes that unconditional positive regard is essential to healthy development. People who have not been exposed to it may come to see themselves in the negative ways that others have made them feel. Through receiving unconditional positive regard, people accept and take responsibility for themselves.

Rogers' unconditional positive regard is essential to helping a fostered or adopted child heal. Rogers believed that it is essential for therapists to show unconditional positive regard to their clients. He also suggested that individuals who don't have this type of acceptance from people in their life can eventually come to hold negative beliefs about themselves.

Fostered and adopted children do not seem to have received unconditional positive regard from their biological parents. That is why it has always been my goal to provide this for them in a corrective emotional experience. I cannot think of a more appropriate time when unconditional positive regard needs to be used to create change than with an abused fostered or adopted child or teen. I have used unconditional positive regard with every fostered or adopted child I have counseled and it works each and every time.

The bottom line is that every child and every human being for that matter needs to feel worthy and appreciated in order to have high self-esteem. This is where your relationship with a fostered or adopted child or teen should begin and end. Unconditional positive regard teaches a person and a child to value themselves. When they value themselves, they tend to make healthy decisions about their future.

It is critical that a fostered or adopted child has a strong sense of security while in your care. There will be times when they will make mistakes and disappoint you. Every child has these moments. What you have to make sure of is that you let the child know through your words and actions that you will still be there for them unconditionally when they make a mistake. Please also make them aware that you will not reject or abandon them. This is their biggest fear. If you do not show the child unconditional positive regard then you will be heading down a very dangerous road of unhealthy attachment.

CHAPTER 5

Strategies for Working with Traumatized Fostered or Adopted Children and Teens

I mentioned earlier in the book that most fostered and adopted children and teens are traumatized children and teens. All of the fostered and adopted children and teens that I have worked with have experienced some kind of trauma within their lives. I have seen firsthand how trauma has led them down a path of feeling rejected, abandoned, unwanted, unloved and unworthy. All of these feelings can lead to low self-esteem. These children had not been given the opportunity to explore their environments. Many of the children who came into my office had never played with a toy and did not know what a book was. They certainly did not know what they were feeling or if they did they did not know how to put words to their emotions. They experienced a great deal of deprivation in their early years which often leads to a failure to thrive. Many of the children did not know how to make decisions for themselves and were unable to identify anything about themselves that was positive.

If you take anything away from this book, I want you to know that even though fostered and adopted children may come to you with low self-esteem, they are wonderful children who need to and can be re-parented in a healthy way to rebuild their self-esteem. It can be done. I have done it with hundreds of fostered and adopted children. You can do the same with a positive attitude and effective tools.

I want you to remember that a fostered or adopted child's sense of self comes from your ability to encourage and support their growth into successful adults. Remember Rome was not built in a day and neither will an abused fostered or adopted child's self-esteem. It takes time and dedication on your part to make this reality come true but, through offering unconditional positive regard, you, as the foster or adoptive parent or professional, have the power to help the child change.

You can begin this change process by:

- accepting where you are at the moment

- making a commitment to move with your fostered or adopted child toward the future

- accepting uncertainty and being open to challenges and change.

Foster and adoptive parents have a very difficult task when it comes to caring for the child. They often report the struggles that they experience with the fostered or adopted child and cannot understand why love is not enough to help the child adjust and move forward with their lives. As discussed in Chapter 4, the truth is that love is not enough. Children need much more than love to form a healthy attachment with others.

I always tell parents who are thinking of becoming a foster or adoptive parent that the role they will be taking on will feel for a long time like a very difficult, draining job. This is not to scare potential foster or adoptive parents away from giving a child a "forever home." It is simply providing them with the truth in order to prepare themselves for a journey of many twists and turns. When potential foster or adoptive parents fool themselves into thinking that this is going to be an easy process of attaching and building a healthy and rewarding relationship with the children, they are setting themselves up for failure. I speak from experience when I say this, as I have seen this happen over and over again to foster and adoptive parents. This lack of understanding on the parents' part about the fostered or adopted child's transition, from the beginning of their involvement, is one of the main causes of multiple placements for children.

Your Self-Evaluation

It is essential for potential foster or adoptive parents to do a self-evaluation to decide if they are willing to take on the commitment of raising a fostered or adopted child. This evaluation should include questions about their role in parenting a traumatized child and has to be concluded first before the parent is ready to help build the child's self-esteem. Let's explore this now. We will then learn ways that you can successfully build the child's self-esteem.

In my expert opinion, successful foster and adoptive parents have the following traits:

- great inner strength and belief in their ability to parent

- the ability to make commitments to others

- positive sense of self

- the ability to self-regulate their emotions, having healed from any trauma of their own

- the ability to put the child's needs before their own

- a not-giving-up attitude

- unconditional positive regard and empathy for others

- a willingness to guide and support the child through difficult times

- a strong support system and the capability to know when to turn to someone for help

- patience, dedication and a willingness to accept mistakes

- a view of the child as a survivor of circumstances

- a willingness to accept that for a while the child will view them as their enemy and reject them on virtually every attempt they make to help them

- the belief that things will improve over time as trust builds

- a willingness to accept their mistakes and learn from them

- understanding that the child's rejection of them is part of their healing process and the ability not to take it personally

- a view of themselves as a tool of empowerment to guide the child towards success.

I have also found that parents who are not as successful connecting with fostered or adopted children have the following traits:

- lack of belief within themselves in their ability to parent a traumatized child

- lack of commitment to people and things

- lack of proper education before fostering or adopting a child (were not provided with specific training on how to manage attachment building, rejection and behavioral issues)

- a misconception that the child has not suffered prior trauma and that their love is enough to create change

- feelings of powerlessness

- the feeling that they lack control over their own life

- unresolved loss issues

- a view of the child as a victim of their circumstances

- a lack of a positive support system

- becoming overwhelmed easily

- not having healed from their own trauma

- lack of control over their own choices

- desire to have instant gratification

- difficulty regulating emotions

- an unwillingness to accept that mistakes will happen

- a belief that the child is acting out to hurt them rather than understanding the child is grieving the loss of their family

- lack of patience and empathy.

It is critical to remember that an abused or neglected fostered or adopted child is a hurt child. They have been stripped of healthy attachments and a sense of self. Their early years of development are the crucial times when they begin to learn about their self-awareness and the fact that they exist and also "matter" to others. Children who were abused during this time do not develop this critical self-awareness. They are coming into foster care with a negative sense of self, feelings of rejection, abandonment and a lack of trust for others. A parent or professional taking on this task of nurturing the child towards a healthy attachment must be cognizant of the work ahead and accepting of the turmoil that comes with the job.

If you are a foster or adoptive parent who has characteristics that fit into the not-as-successful parenting category, or you are working with parents with these characteristics, there is hope for becoming successful. It first begins with recognizing that you need to change your parenting skills. You can begin your journey with implementing the skills you are going to learn throughout this book. If you do not give up on yourself, the children will not give up on you. Remember you are the child's best role model.

Putting Yourself in the Child or Teen's Shoes Leads to Bonding

I will never forget the day a 13-year-old foster child said to me, "Dr. Sue, you never walked in my shoes. You grew up with a mom and a dad who loved you and you are lucky. I didn't. I got cheated and was thrown out like a piece of trash. You know what that feels like? It feels like nobody wants you, so why should I even want myself?"

That was the day I realized two important aspects of helping fostered and adopted children and teens become successful and build high self-esteem. I realized (1) that rejection causes these children to have low self-esteem and (2) that if I was going to make any progress with these children, I had to allow them to take me on their personal journey and help me to walk in their shoes.

After the child left my office that day, I was filled with overwhelming emotions. I had to process what happened in that session. I took some time to visualize what that child's life was like growing up. I imagined how sad she must have felt carrying the feeling of being unwanted around with her every day of her life. No child should have to carry that burden. Yet she was not the only foster child feeling that way day in and day out. In fact, she was in the majority when it comes to foster children. I learned that as I continued counseling more children. I knew that if I wanted to help these innocent children build a life filled with confidence, this was where my work had to begin with them. I had to show them that they were worthy of acceptance, love and nurturance. However, to do this, I had to get inside their world and learn what it was like to have lived their pain. This is exactly what you need to do as well if you want to make a big difference in a fostered or adopted child's life. They will reject you at first; however, the less you push and the more you listen, the further you will move along in the bonding process.

When a child feels that they are a mistake, they tend to feel worthless, alone and depressed. These are symptoms for both fostered and adopted children. The child therefore has no desire to work towards building positive self-esteem because they feel that no one cares. Their pain has to be validated and acknowledged in order for them to move beyond the pain. This is where the technique of "joining" is critical to connecting with the child. Joining occurs when you simply agree with their feelings. You do not say to the child that they are wrong for feeling this way. You say, "You have every right to feel the way you do."

I have used joining with every child I have counseled and it is quite effective in beginning to build a trusting relationship with the child. Think about this for a minute: when you are feeling angry about something, do you want someone telling you to be happy? I don't. I want my anger acknowledged. I want an ally in my misery. I want someone who understands how I am feeling. When I receive that response, I feel that someone understands me and that is the person I know I can go to when I need help. Fostered and adopted children want the same thing. Be the child's ally in their healing and show them that you are able to take a walk in their shoes. Knowing that someone "gets" you helps you to feel good about yourself.

As I said at the beginning of the book, I have often questioned how some other clinicians provided treatment to the fostered or adopted children they were counseling. I have always been an innovator, trying different strategies outside traditional therapy techniques when it comes to working with children. I remember being a child myself and feeling depressed and confused at times about situations in my life. I often thought, "I just wish that there was someone out there who could understand what I am feeling." I did not want someone to tell me I was wrong about how I was feeling. I wanted someone to say, "Kid, you have every right to be angry, sad and confused." I wanted to know that I was not alone in my pain. That is what I believe every child wants when they are hurting and that is why I meet every child that comes into my office in the same way. My philosophy is that understanding creates connections. Unless I start failing at this with fostered and adopted children, I am going to continue to use it.

The only way I believe that fostered or adopted children can be helped is if you see things from their perspective. If you can manage to parent or provide professional help to a fostered or adopted child from this perspective then you can truly make a difference in these kids' lives and truly build a lasting relationship. I know what foster parents are thinking right now, "How can I build a lasting relationship with a child if they are just going to be reunited with their biological parents?" The answer to this is quite simple, "For the time the child is with you, you can give them the gift of empathy, patience and understanding, that they will take with them for the rest of their lives."

With foster children's help, I have walked in many of their shoes. The walk was sometimes grueling, painful and long. I accomplished this by getting to know each and every one of them on their terms. I listened when the child wanted to talk and backed off when they said that today was not the day to talk. I promised, yes, promised, that for the time that I was there with them, I would give 100 percent of myself and I did. When a child said to me, "You will just leave me like every other therapist or person I know," I responded by saying, "You have every right to think that based on the fact that you could not count on the people who were supposed to never leave you. I guess then it will be my job to prove I will be different." If you make the choice to have a foster child live in your home or make a commitment to adopt a foster child, it will be your job to prove to the child that you are different from their biological parents.

I'd like to conclude this chapter with a story about a very special foster child who taught me the true meaning of walking in her shoes. This child's story changed the way I practiced therapy with fostered and adopted children. She helped me to see that bonding with a traumatized child is a give-and-take relationship. I learned that foster children have a great deal to give and that underneath all of their sadness and pain they want what any child desires, love, support and a place to call home.

It was as if a ball of thunder rolled into my office on that cold winter day. There was a fire in her eyes that could have burnt a house to the ground. I said, "Hello." She replied, "Who you talking to?" I replied, "I don't see anyone else here, so I guess that would be you." She replied, "You are just like every other therapist I have ever had. You are here for the money. (*Inside I laughed at that since I was making about minimum wage at the time.*) You don't care about me." Before I could get a word in, she went on to say, "The last therapist told me that she didn't care if I talked to her or not she was still going to get paid for the hour." My response to this was, "Well, that therapist is a total idiot and should be fired." That got her attention. She said, "You are not allowed to say that." I replied, "Well, I just did and I will say it again." Before I could, she said, "You are different, aren't you? Where did you come from?" I gave her my home address and she laughed.

Coco never missed a session with me after that day. Don't get me wrong, it was an uphill battle for a while between Coco and me. We were both struggling at times to have power in the relationship. However, I soon realized that by letting go of some of my authoritative power, I allowed her to feel less threatened. You see, foster children expect you to reject them simply because they experienced rejection from other adults, their biological parents. They are so good at pushing you to your limits and pushing you away. It really is a defense mechanism to protect themselves from further pain and abandonment. They want to control you so you do not control them and hurt them as they have already been hurt. To the foster child, you represent every adult who has ever rejected them. You also represent adults who have taken them away from their biological parents and put them into foster care. Yes, even though their biological parents abused and/or neglected them, they still long to be with them. That loyalty must be acknowledged and honored by you, if you want to create a healthy relationship with your fostered or adopted child. You must never pretend that your fostered or adopted child's previous life, biological parents or siblings never existed. If you make the mistake of doing so, you will lose the child forever and they are likely to end up resenting you.

To be perfectly honest, rejection is a smart defense for a foster child. It reminds me of the concept of fight or flight. The fight-or-flight response, also known as the acute stress response, refers to a physiological reaction that occurs in the presence of something that is terrifying, either mentally or physically. The fight-or-flight response was first described in the 1920s by American physiologist Walter Cannon. Cannon (1994) realized that a chain of rapidly occurring reactions inside the body help mobilize the body's resources to deal with threatening circumstances. In layman's terms, fight or flight simply means you face a traumatic situation head on or you run from your fear because the feelings are so overwhelming. Foster children mostly flee from their fears (and so they avoid getting close to another person that they believe will leave) because their emotional feelings of connecting are so terrifying. Fear is guided by the child's perception of what is frightening. So, if a foster child perceives that you will leave them, even if it is not true, their perception is what triggers their flight response.

Knowing that foster children are afraid to trust, it is our job to teach them that not everyone leaves. It is also critical to teach them that sometimes people do not stay forever as well. The best advice I can share with you in the beginning of your connection process with your fostered or adopted child is that you accept where they are in their healing process. That starting point is often a place of rejection. If you are patient and you learn the skills needed to connect, you will slowly build a bond with the child. This is what occurred between children such as Coco and myself. During the time that we spent together in therapy, I often let her take the lead as I followed. It is hard to let go of the power that comes with being an adult over a child. Foster and adoptive parents share that sentiment with me very often. I completely understand their feelings. I also always remind them that when you are raised by an adult who did not exert proper parenting power over you, you certainly have no clue about how to accept a parent who is setting rules and boundaries with you. That feels completely foreign, smothering and intrusive to a child who has never had that experience before.

CHAPTER 6

Assessing Your Parenting and Professional Skills

Self-Evaluation: Do You Have What it Takes to Help Your Fostered or Adopted Child or Teen Increase Their Self-Esteem?

In the remainder of this book, I will teach you how to begin the process of connecting with your fostered or adopted child or teen on a healthy supportive level while moving them towards healthy self-esteem. This process, however, begins with looking at yourself and where you are with your own level of self-worth.

A child's self-esteem is acquired, not inherited. It is developed through your consistency in valuing your child as they develop. In order to help a child build their self-esteem, it helps if you have a high level of self-confidence. Children observe this confidence in adults and will model it. Likewise, if a child is raised by a parent with low self-esteem they mirror that as well.

Low self-esteem can negatively affect virtually every facet of your life, including your relationships, your job and your health. But you can take steps to boost your self-esteem, even if you've been holding a poor opinion of yourself since childhood. If there are difficulties in your past that are affecting your current ability to parent a child, then I suggest you confront them. Dr. Sears (2011) suggests the following steps to help you build your self-esteem:

1. Parents are not perfect and make a great deal of mistakes. If you think about it, they probably did their best given how they were parented. However, Sears makes it clear that if your parents were abusive towards you, you do not forget what happened to you but you try to forgive them in order to move forward with your life. It has been shown, even in my own work with abuse survivors, that once children can confront their shame and embarrassment from the abuse they free themselves from the chains their parents have wrapped around them.

2. In the early years, a child's sense of self is mostly determined by their parents' emotional states as they are the child's primary role models. Sears also claims that children tend to pick up on what their parents are sending out emotionally. For example, if you are anxious, your child will internalize this emotion. Likewise, if you are happy, they will reflect that emotion. Children often translate your unhappiness with yourself to mean unhappiness with them. Even infants know they are supposed to please their parents. As they get older, they may even come to feel responsible for their parents' happiness. If you are not content, they think they must not be good (or good enough). If you are experiencing severe anxiety or depression, you should seek proper treatment, so it does not affect your child's development.

3. Children's self-image often develops from how they think others see them. Sears claims that this is especially true in preschoolers, who learn about themselves from their parent's reactions. Ask yourself these questions: Do you reflect positive or negative images to your child? Do you let your child know that their thoughts are important to you? It is important to remember that when your child receives positive reinforcements from you, they begin to

think positively about themselves. Sears also claims that your child will look to your to correct their negative behavior as well.

4.   Be realistic. On this, Sears says:

> You can't be up and smiling all the time and still be human. Your child should know that parents have down days, too. Children can see through fake cheerfulness. Your sensitivity toward him will increase his sensitivity toward you, and someday he may be the one lifting your self-confidence.

If you do not feel secure about yourself, how on earth are you going to help a child build their self-esteem? It takes a confident human being to encourage a child to feel good about themselves. After all, as I said before, parents and caregivers are their child's best role models. If the child or teen does not see you as having confidence, then how are they going to trust in you to help them? They have to believe that you have the confidence to help them gain confidence.

I could not accomplish all of the amazing work I do with fostered and adopted children and teens without feeling good about myself. Every time I have walked in to counsel a foster or adopted child, I have entered the room thinking, "I can change this child's life for the better." I never resented the hard days. I embraced them, simply because it gave me more fuel to figure out what I had to do to break through to the child.

I presented at a conference about a month ago and a therapist asked me afterwards if everyone can apply the techniques that I was teaching. My response was that they can, but it depends on three important factors: (1) your level of self-confidence, (2) your passion to make a difference in a fostered or adopted child's life and (3) your belief that you have the ability to help a fostered or adopted child have a better life and your desire to do so.

Every one of us has a little voice inside our head guiding us. Sometimes the voice is positive and sometimes it is negative. I am a true believer that each one of us has the ability to change our negative voice into a positive one. This takes practice, dedication and a desire to live a life of purpose. If you believe that your purpose is to provide a fostered or adopted child with a second chance at life, then you must be in a positive healthy place to do so. If you are not, then please do the "self work" you need to do to get ready. The last thing that these children need is more abandonment and disappointment.

Your Role in Helping Fostered or Adopted Children Build Self-Esteem

Let's begin your journey of helping a fostered or adopted child or teen build self-confidence by looking at where you stand with your self-esteem. Please complete the following chart. Check off each box that applies to your current state of self-worth. Please be honest in your response.

Do you often...?

think that you can't accomplish a specific goal ☐

think that you can't handle your feelings ☐

worry that things will not work out ☐

tell yourself, "I am not strong enough to handle this" ☐

feel fear of the unknown ☐

avoid making changes in your life ☐

have trouble putting yourself forward ☐

constantly need reassurance ☐

feel resentment ("It's so much easier for others") ☐

If you answered "Yes" to almost all of the questions above, you have some work to do on yourself to get to a place where you can be the best role model to your fostered or adopted child or teen. The good news is that there are some simple skills that you can build quickly to get started. According to Butler and Hope (2007), there are six strategies for building self-confidence. Butler and Hope believe, as do I, that confidence is not just one thing, it is many things. In addition, confidence comes from doing things. It comes from taking actions to improve who you are. These are the six strategies:

1. Practice: You have to make building your self-confidence a habit. The more you think about being confident the more you will present as confident and assured.

2. Behave "as if": Ask yourself: How would I behave if I really felt confident? How would I look, feel and walk? How would I handle specific situations?

3. Take the zig-zag path: No one builds self-confidence over night. Also, no one is confident in every situation. You will experience ups and downs and a zig-zag path.

4. Make the most of your mistakes and then ignore them: The mistake made by unconfident people is to think that mistakes matter. They do matter to some degree but everyone fails and errors are made for learning. When you make a mistake, try again.

5. Limit the self-blame: Kicking yourself for past inadequacies, confusions or failures gives fuel to your internal negative voice. Stop doing this and use an encouraging voice instead. Amplify encouraging messages to yourself until you hear them loud and clear.

6. Be kind to yourself: Stop punishing yourself and start treating yourself with self-respect. Your self-worth will grow and grow.

I love Butler and Hope's six suggestions for building self-esteem, because they are practical and easy to accomplish as long as you put in the work. If you can implement these six strategies, then they will also give you the tools to guide your child or teen to success.

Another suggestion that I have for parents who are struggling to help their fostered or adopted children build their self-worth is to look at their daily "internal dialogue" about their foster or adopted child. Our internal dialogue guides our actions towards ourselves and the people around us, including our kids.

Some parents experience an internal dialogue which says:

1. I can't do this anymore.

2. I give up. I did not sign up to take on a kid with all these problems.

3. I want to give this kid back.

They are not parenting from a positive place. Rather, these parents are stuck in a negative thinking pattern which will only bring negativity. If you tell yourself that you will fail, you will. The problem with having a negative internal dialogue when parenting a traumatized fostered or adopted child is that you are not only disappointing yourself but you are also making a choice to disappoint a child who has been failed already.

If your message to yourself is negative about the situation with your fostered or adopted child, there is good news. You have the ability within yourself to change your thinking from negative to positive. However, this takes dedication, a great deal of education and a willingness to recognize that you are sad beneath your anger because the child is not listening or bonding with you. You see, under frustration and anger lies sadness. Sadness that you cannot reach the child with whom you want to connect.

I hear from so many frustrated foster and adoptive parents who say, "I've tried everything to help my child succeed and nothing works. I'm frustrated and I can't do this anymore." To me, the word "can't" means "won't." When you tell yourself that you can't help your fostered or adopted child succeed, then you are saying that you will not prepare yourself to make a change to help the child. Your message to yourself is negative which in turn causes you low self-esteem. Remember that when you have low self-esteem and are not feeling positive about yourself and your ability to parent, the child picks up on this and internalizes it. When you are parenting from an empowering positive place, the child will emulate that.

I am not for self-blame. When we take this negative approach to ourselves, we are telling ourselves we are not good enough. Where does that get you? Nowhere. I understand that parenting a fostered or adopted child or teen is extremely challenging and very difficult. I even understand foster and adoptive parents feeling sometimes that they "wish they never took this child into their home or adopted the child." These are very normal feelings to have along this journey. It is okay to think these thoughts. It is okay to feel these feelings. It is never okay to verbalize these feelings and thoughts to the child. If you let your frustration overcome you and share your raw emotions with the child, you are further adding to the child's already low self-esteem.

There were many days in session with these children where I felt frustrated and sad because I was not making as much progress with the child as I had hoped for. There were days where I wanted to scream, "Why did I ever take this job? I can't make a difference in these kids' lives." Instead of internalizing these feelings or stating them to the child, I found an outlet to release these feelings. I turned to my supervisor for support. You need to find a place to turn for support as well. This may be a friend, spouse or a journal. The moment you let the tension and frustration build without releasing it, you are entering into crisis mode and heading towards negative thinking and actions.

If you have been guilty of self-blame and negative thinking about your situation with your fostered or adopted child or teen, stop punishing yourself for this and find a way to move forward. Remember, you are most likely becoming frustrated when you feel helpless. If you build the skills to feel powerful in your role as the parent and guide for your child you will not get to the point of negative thinking. Remember, the child already feels helpless and that is the last thing we want them to experience from their foster or adoptive parent. Parents who succeed with fostered or adopted children empower themselves to rid themselves of negative thinking and insert positive thinking.

It is important to realize that if you are becoming frustrated and angry with your child, it only means that the approach you are taking is not working. It does not mean that the child is incapable of bonding with you. It means that you have to learn new ways to reach the child. As a parent and a person, you have more control than you think in helping the child build high self-esteem.

Your sense of control begins with you (1) recognizing that the child is not trying to make you mad on purpose but simply does not know another way to behave, (2) learning to control your reactions and (3) finding an outlet for your anger.

At times you must think of yourself as a problem solver (Butler and Hope, 2007).

1. You have to identify the issue you are struggling with in terms of your child.

2. You have to recognize that there is a difficulty.

3. You then have to make a choice to learn and implement new strategies to help connect with your child.

4. You then have to come up with a plan.

Here is an example to guide you through the problem-solving process.

1. Identify the issue: My adopted child curses at me and has been saying, "I'm not your real son." You feel rejection.

2. Recognize the difficulty: My son is having difficulty bonding with me because he is afraid that I may abandon or reject him based on his knowledge of his biological parents. This is his reality and I respect it.

3. Make a choice to learn a new strategy: I am aware that my son is struggling. I have made a decision to seek help and learn how to approach this subject with my son in a way that means he feels supported and validated.

4. Come up with a plan: I will ask for a referral to a therapist who can help guide us through this roadblock.

If you can master these suggestions, you will change your way of reacting negatively and start seeing changes not only in yourself but also, more importantly, in your relationship with your child. Isn't that what every parent wants with their child, a strong, meaningful, respectful relationship?

You always have a "choice" as to whether you want to go down a road of destructiveness or a road of rebuilding. Fostered and adopted children and teens need you to take effective action to help them build high self-esteem. When they see that you are trying to encourage instead of criticizing, they internalize that as you caring enough about them to help. We all feel better about ourselves when we know that someone is in our corner cheering us along. Fostered and adopted children and teens need you to be their cheerleader!

I have found that foster and adoptive parents who are most successful in helping their child to build a healthy sense of self have a positive internal dialogue going on within themselves even when things go wrong. These parents say to themselves:

1. I have made a choice to foster or adopt this child and I will do anything I can to help them succeed.

2. I may want to give up on some days but I will not because, if I do, what message is that saying to this vulnerable child? That no one wants them.

3. I will always put this child's needs before myself. It does not matter if they are my blood relation or not.

4. I decided to take this foster child into my home and I will do everything in my power to help them while they are here.

Become this positive force within a fostered or adopted child's life!

CHAPTER 7

Strategies for Increasing Fostered or Adopted Children and Teens' Self-Esteem

There are numerous strategies that can be implemented to increase a fostered or adopted child or teen's self-esteem. In this chapter I will share with you the skills and tools that have worked best for me with these children over the years. They include (1) seeing the child as a survivor, (2) building resiliency, (3) instilling self-determination, (4) increasing motivation and (5) creating a sense of belonging.

Seeing the Fostered or Adopted Child as a "Survivor" not a "Victim"

Early on in my career in working with fostered or adopted children, I felt sorry for what each child had to endure. I had sympathy for these children. I later learned that I needed to have empathy for the children to move them forward with their lives. I had to hold back my pity about what had happened to them and develop an understanding of their situation. I had to let them know that I would also be feeling alone, scared and sad if I had not been able to live with my biological family. I had to let them know that I did not feel sorry for them but I felt sad that they had an unfair start in life. I also wanted them to know that what had occurred in their young lives did not have to define who they would become. I helped each child to understand that they had a choice to form an identity that they were proud of.

Truth be told, abused and neglected children are victims of their parents' incapability to care for their needs properly. It is perfectly fine to acknowledge this to yourself. However, it is more important to see the child as a "survivor" and not a victim. The children survived their parents' abuse and in many instances incorporated coping skills into their daily routines to live through the abuse they were experiencing. We see this in the form of defense mechanisms that these children implemented while living within their birth homes. As therapists or foster/ adoptive parents, we see these children's survival techniques in the form of hoarding, denying themselves closeness with others and lying.

It has been my experience that when a child or an adult views themselves as a victim, they believe that they do not deserve nice things and are filled with low self-esteem, shame and confusion. Furthermore, victims often feel alone, hopeless, often believe that everyone is better or stronger, live in the past and are uncomfortable around others, especially therapists.

When a child or an adult learns to become a survivor of their circumstances instead of a victim, they begin to feel proud and live in the here and now. They begin to feel hope that their life can be more than they believed it could be. They slowly begin to have gratitude for life, slowly open up to people they believe can be trusted. They begin to laugh again, look towards the future, understand that emotional pain passes and begin to feel whole and authentic.

I don't know about you but I would rather live as a survivor than a victim. Seeing oneself as a victim stops you in your tracks from moving forward. Viewing yourself as a survivor moves you forward. Becoming a survivor I believe is most critical for children who have been unjustly victimized. Children are young and vulnerable but extremely resilient. They have their whole lives in front of them to live. What has happened to them at five, six or seven years old does not have to affect the rest of their lives. That is the thinking approach I have always worked from while counseling fostered or adopted children. (It is also my approach to helping adults.) When you see a fostered or adopted child as a survivor you acknowledge that they have resiliency to heal.

Resiliency

I am a firm believer in resiliency. I strongly believe that it is the key to having high self-esteem. Resiliency is the process of adapting well in the face of adversity, trauma, tragedy, threats or significant sources of stress—such as family and relationship problems, serious health problems or workplace and financial stressors. It means "bouncing back" from difficult experiences. Resiliency is the capacity to withstand stress and catastrophe. Psychologists have long recognized the capabilities of humans to adapt and overcome risk and adversity. Individuals and communities are able to rebuild their lives even after devastating tragedies (Alvord *et al.*, 2003).

Being resilient doesn't mean going through life without experiencing stress and pain. People feel grief, sadness and a range of other emotions after adversity and loss. The road to resiliency lies in working through the emotions and effects of stress and painful events.

Resiliency is not something that you're either born with or not. Resiliency develops as people grow up and gain better thinking and self-management skills and more knowledge. Resiliency also comes from supportive relationships with parents, peers and others, as well as cultural beliefs and traditions that help people cope with the inevitable bumps in life. Resiliency is found in a variety of behaviors, thoughts and actions that can be learned and developed across the life span (Alvord *et al.*, 2003).

In my years of working with fostered and adopted children, I have always been amazed by the resiliency that so many of these children have despite the circumstances they suffered. Many fostered or adopted children are emotionally strong, despite the fact that they were victims of circumstances. I often find myself asking, "Why do some of these children become so resilient while others fall through the cracks?" The answer seems to be a combination of pure inner strength, an innate desire to survive and the influence of a positive person in the fostered or adopted child's life.

Some foster children survive their circumstances by stuffing their feelings deep down inside themselves. Many of us may not agree with this coping technique; however, if you think of it as a protective defense against further pain, you may change your mind. The child's feelings are something that no one can touch or take away. It becomes their solitude. Although it is painful for them to carry these misunderstood feelings with them, it is something that gives them strength. Their feelings are something none can take from them.

Many fostered and adopted children also have an innate desire to survive the circumstances that are thrown at them. Some foster children may just manifest this ability. It is a part of their genetic make-up. They believe that things will get better and they will survive. Many children in the system have confided in me that they always felt they were more than just a child in foster care. They believed that there was more to them than the label they were given by the system.

It should be clear to you that fostered and adopted children are victims of circumstances. These children did nothing to cause the abuse, neglect or abandonment that they have suffered. Adopted children did nothing wrong to be placed for adoption by their birth parents. Yet both adopted and fostered children often feel that they are the cause of everything that went wrong. In the case of abused children, this feeling is often caused by messages that they were sent while they were being abused. For example, I remember one of the foster teens with whom I worked telling me, "My mother told me I was the worst mistake she ever had. What am I supposed to do with that? I believed her for a very long time."

Approaching a fostered or adopted child or teen as a victim is not always the best way to help them move forward with their life and build a healthy sense of self. Approaching a fostered or adopted child or teen with the mindset that you can encourage and lead them to live a proud and respected life is where the trauma treatment should begin. I am not saying for one moment that you should not acknowledge their suffering. I always begin by telling the child that what led them to be in foster care or adopted was not their fault. I also answer their questions as honestly as possible about their past. I encourage you to do this as well. However, my goal in acknowledging their suffering is not to have them define themselves as a victim. When one does this, one may stay stuck in that role of wanting people to pity or feel bad for what they experienced. I have found that this is *not* what children and teens want from others who are trying to help them. I acknowledge what happened to the fostered or adopted child in order to teach them to gain strength from it. I have found that they want someone to empower them to move beyond the pain and build a strong identity for themselves.

Sirota (2010) gives a great summary of why it is important for children not to remain victims of circumstances. Sirota claims that an essential part of being an adult involves taking responsibility for ourselves. This means making conscious, empowered choices on our own behalf. Children aren't capable of doing this when they are very young because they are too helpless to understand or deal with all the things happening to them. Children need the adults in their lives to care for them and protect them from harm. Abused children also need someone to guide them beyond their abusive past and lead them toward an empowered life.

Sirota also believes that adult survivors of emotional child abuse have only two life-choices: learn to build resiliency or remain a victim. When your self-concept has been shredded, when you have been deeply injured and made to feel the injury was all your fault, when you look for approval to those who cannot or will not provide it—you play the role assigned to you by your abusers. I believe that for fostered or adopted children or teens, that it is time to stop playing that role, time to write their own script. Victims of abuse carry the cure in their own hearts and souls. For the emotionally abused child, healing *does* come down to "forgiveness"—forgiveness of yourself (Vachss, 1994).

Building Resiliency

There are several tips that professionals and parents can use to help a fostered or adopted child or teen build resiliency. As I have said throughout this book, all of this occurs much faster if you can build a positive attachment to the child. Children who experience chronic adversity fare better or recover more successfully when they have a positive relationship with a competent adult, they are good learners and problem solvers, and they have areas of competence and perceived efficacy valued by self or society (Masten, Best and Garmezy, 1990).

You must believe that abused and neglected fostered or adopted children and teens can build resiliency despite what has happened to them in order to move them towards a healthy sense of self. The ability to adapt well to adversity, trauma, tragedy, threats or other significant sources of stress can help our children manage stress and feelings of anxiety and uncertainty. However, being resilient does not mean that children won't experience difficulty or distress. Emotional pain and sadness are common when we have suffered major trauma or personal loss, or even when we hear of someone else's loss or trauma.

We can all develop resiliency, and we can help our fostered and adopted children develop it as well. It involves behaviors, thoughts and actions that can be learned over time. I would now like to give you some tips on how to begin building resiliency in fostered or adopted children. Below you will find a list of strategies I have implemented with these children. You can implement them as well.

1. Teach Fostered or Adopted Children and Teens Empathy

Teach your fostered or adopted child the skill of empathy, or feeling another's pain. This can occur slowly in the beginning of the process and should begin with you having empathy for the child. Remember that you are the child's best role model. Encourage your child to be a friend in order to get friends. Build a strong family network to support your child through their inevitable disappointments and hurts. At school, watch to make sure that your child is not being isolated. Connecting with people provides social support and strengthens resiliency.

2. Encourage Your Fostered or Adopted Children and Teens to Help Others

Fostered and adopted children who may feel helpless can be empowered by helping others. Have your child help you with some task that they can master. Make them a part of projects that you are doing; include them in helping others obtain their goals. Reciprocity is a big self-esteem booster for kids. It gives them confidence to know that they have the power within themselves to help others change. In turn, you will see them applying that same power to themselves.

3. Help Your Fostered or Adopted Children and Teens to Maintain a daily routine

Sticking to a routine can be comforting to children, especially children who have never had structure in their lives. It helps the child to feel safe. Encourage your child to develop their own routines. Children who are abused or neglected prior to coming into care probably had little to no structure. It is hard to relearn structure and takes patience on your part, but it can and must be accomplished to help fostered or adopted children build resiliency and self-esteem. Learning and maintaining structure in one's life is also essential for latter development in terms of schooling and work. An example of a positive daily routine to start this process would be: Waking up, brushing teeth, eating breakfast, saying a positive goodbye to each other, going to school, returning from school, downtime, homework, dinner, downtime/homework, bedtime.

4. Teach Fostered or Adopted Children and Teens to Take a Break

If your child is worrying, teach them how to focus on something besides what's worrying them. If your child suffered abuse before you fostered or adopted them, do not make your early bonding experience about the abuse. This of course needs to be a part of your bonding process but remember you must develop trust before any of the real exploration of trauma and healing can begin. Be aware of what your child is exposed to. If they were abused, take a break from television shows that depict this kind of information. In addition, do not put your child in an overwhelming situation that they are not ready for. I have seen parents, not by their own fault, enroll fostered or adopted children in social activities that may feel overwhelming to a child who has low self-esteem. You may believe that this can be helpful on the surface but it can end up being hurtful to the child when they do not yet possess the ability to make friends. It's just a good plan to "take a break" from the trauma in the beginning of your bonding process and spend time together doing activities.

5. Teach Your Fostered or Adopted Children and Teens Self-Care

Make yourself a good example, and teach your child the importance of making time to eat properly, exercise and rest. Make sure your child has time to have fun, and make sure that your child hasn't scheduled every moment of their life with no "downtime" to relax. Caring for oneself and having fun will help your child stay balanced and deal better with stressful times. I am a firm believer that parents and professionals have to be a child's best role model. Children imitate what they observe. From a very young age, children are like sponges, soaking up everything that they are seeing. Be a role model that your children can admire and emulate. Being a positive role model in your children's lives consists of showing them to be kind, giving and sensitive human beings to themselves and others. Sometimes, we tend to forget these very important emotional aspects of development. Remember, being kind to yourself first teaches you how to be kind to others. Your children are watching you very closely. They are observing how you act, behave and relate to others. They are incorporating your values and beliefs. Remember you have a tremendous power to direct your children on a positive path to becoming successful individuals. When you show your children that they can care successfully for themselves, you are teaching them to build self-reliance.

6. Teach Your Fostered or Adopted Children and Teens to Move Towards Goals

Teach your child to set reasonable goals and then to move toward them one step at a time. For example, in working with fostered or adopted children, I never began treatment with big goals for the kids to accomplish. Instead I set up small goals that would help them reach bigger goals. Many fostered or adopted children have unresolved feelings pent up inside that they have extreme difficulty expressing all at once. Knowing that releasing these feelings is healing for these children, I have to find ways to help them release the emotions slowly over time. So, I usually start off only asking the child or teen to state the feelings connected to being separated from their family. From there, I may move on to asking them to put a story to the feelings. Eventually, taking baby steps to accomplish big steps, the child will, it is hoped, be able to talk more freely about their feelings about being separated from their biological family members and home. It's not how fast you get a child to express their feelings here, it is that you accomplish it at their pace with dedicated acceptance and patience on your part. Moving toward that goal—even if it's a tiny step—and receiving praise for doing so will focus your child on what they have accomplished rather than on what hasn't been accomplished, and can help build the resiliency to move forward in the face of challenges.

7. Nurture a Positive Self-View in Your Fostered or Adopted Child or Teen

Help your fostered or adopted child or teen remember ways that they have successfully handled hardships in the past and then help them understand that these past challenges can help them build the strength to handle future challenges. This is a great confidence builder. Most fostered or adopted children do not see the positive aspects of their accomplishments. This is often caused by the fact that other adults, prior to their coming into the foster care system, never pointed them out to the child. I think the best way to accomplish this is to remind the child how brave and strong they are to have survived their life circumstances. This is especially helpful for teens but you can begin this process when the child is younger.

8. Teach Your Fostered or Adopted Child or Teen to Make Decisions

Help your child learn to trust themselves to solve problems and make appropriate decisions. One of the big issues fostered and adopted children struggle with is making decisions for themselves. One reason is that most of their decisions have been made for them. It was decided that they would be put up for adoption or removed from their homes and placed into foster care. If you think about it, making decisions for yourself is a learned behavior; however, when you have people making decisions for you all the time, you cannot possibly trust your own feelings or thoughts to be true. Therefore making decisions become very difficult. Most fostered and adopted children and teens with whom I have worked have difficulty making simple decisions such as what color they like. I would often get a response from the child of, "I don't know which color I like." I would then proceed to give them choices. Teaching a fostered or adopted child or teen that they have the ability to make choices shapes their autonomy which in turn builds a positive sense of self. If you want to set your child up for success and prepare them for living independently in a world where the only constant is change, you need to recognize the importance of giving your child choices.

The gift of choice offers children the ability to grow and excel cognitively, emotionally and socially. When you give your child the opportunity to make choices within reasonable limits, you are offering them the chance to learn and master skills necessary for independent living.

By giving your child choices you will:

1. Encourage him to explore consequences to decisions. What happens if I choose to do this by myself instead of waiting for help?

2. Foster a sense of autonomy. As children develop their unique sense of self, they want the power to influence their environment. This is not to be confused with manipulation.

3. Reduce conflicts. Let's face it, no one likes an authority figure standing over their shoulder dictating their every move. Yes, sometimes we need to do things we don't want to do, but your goal is to prepare your child to live and thrive independently in the world, and the reality is that we always have a choice.

4. Teach your child respect. Offering choice shows your child that you value him as a person who is worthy and capable of deciding "What comes next?"

5. Encourage your child to think for himself. Is your goal truly to raise a child who respects authority, or one who blindly obeys authority in order to avoid conflict?

6. Foster creativity. Giving your child the opportunity to make choices enables him to tap into his creativity. This might mean coming up with a new way to play with a toy, or inventing the next great after-school snack.

(Integrated Child, 2013)

Children's ability to make their own decisions is crucial to their latter development. Helping and teaching your child to make their own decisions provides them with a sense of self-worth.

When a child makes a positive decision based on their own thoughts, they can feel pure satisfaction because it was their own choice. Likewise, when a child makes a not so positive decision on their own, they can learn from that choice and try to make a better one next time. Taylor (2009) discusses that it is part of a child's job to sometimes make stupid decisions that we as parents may not agree with and that these decisions is a part of helping them gain maturity. Taylor also concludes that encouraging children to make their own decisions is not extremely easy. This is very true. Children still need guidance and help to make decisions based on their age but, as Taylor suggests, you can begin to teach early decision-making skills over time in small increments. The best way to help a child make a decision is to provide him with choices. For example, you wouldn't tell your children they can have any candy they want in a convenience store. They would be overwhelmed with the choices and paralyzed with indecision, or they would want everything in the store. What you would do is give them a choice between jawbreakers, licorice or bubble gum, and they would then decide which treat they want. By limiting their choices, children tend to feel more in control of their decision making.

Good decision making takes a great deal of time and practice. We often see young children and adolescents making a great deal of impulsive decisions. This occurs simply because they want instant gratification. Taylor suggests that there are several steps that can be taught to children and teens to help them make good decisions. These steps include:

1. Stop before you leap: Try to catch and stop children and teens from making a negative decision. Suggest another positive alternative to them.

2. Question their decisions: When the child or teen does not make a good decision, simply ask them how he could have made a better decision and why he made the decision

he did. It is important that a child or teen realizes what motivates his decisions.

3. Teach options: Children and teens need to know that they have choices when it comes to decision making. Knowing that they do have choices can help them choose the best one.

4. Teach consequences: Children and teens should be able to judge the benefits and the rewards of their decisions. Parents can help them to accomplish this by talking about the possible results of the decision.

9. Helping Your Fostered or Adopted Child Maintain a "Hopeful" Outlook

Even when your fostered or adopted child is facing very painful events, help them look at the situation in a broader context and keep a long-term perspective. Although your child may be too young to consider a long-term perspective on their own, help them see that there is a future beyond the current situation and that the future can be good. An optimistic and positive outlook enables your child to see the good things in life and keep going even in the hardest times (Masten *et al.*, 1990). This is such an important part of a fostered or adopted child's healing process.

The key term to keep in mind in this tip is *hope*. As humans, we *need* hope. We can't live without it. It helps us to survive and move beyond pain. It is also sometimes the only thing that pulls us out of the deep trenches of the pain and hurt of life. Fostered or adopted children need hope to believe that their future will not include all of the pain from the past. These children may also hang on to hope that their parents will get better and come back and take better care of them. For some children this is a reality and that hope should be acknowledged by professionals and parents providing care for them. When termination of parental rights are handed down it often does not take away the child's hope. That hope needs to be discussed openly and honestly with you and the child. It needs to be acknowledged, with the main point being that there is a future beyond the current situation.

I have had the "hopeful" conversation with many fostered and adopted children and teens over the years. Here is an example to help you have the conversation as well:

> "Dylan (*age 11*), I want to talk to you today about your feelings about reuniting with your biological parents. You have been in foster care now for two years and have been living with a foster family that you have reported really liking. We have talked also a great deal about adoption but you said that you were not sure about this move and did not want to give up hope of your mother coming back to get you. I want you to know that you don't have to give up your hope. It could be a reality some day that your mom will return but for now it does not look like that is going to happen. That does not mean in any way that it could never happen. For now, you are in a safe place with people who love you and want to care for you. I don't know what the future may hold for you, you don't either but what I do know is that you deserve to be in a home where you are given every opportunity to grow and develop into a successful young man."

In this example, I want you to notice how "hope" is not removed from Dylan but my language has allowed him to look beyond the current moment and see that the future could be great with a lot of possibilities. The way I delivered that message to Dylan helped him to have a hopeful and positive outlook on his future. In fact, Dylan was adopted six months later by his now permanent family. His adoptive family has kept alive Dylan's hopes of reuniting with his mother by stressing to him that they will not turn away his mother if she wishes to have a relationship with Dylan in the future. Although this offer by Dylan's adoptive parents does not happen for every child and depends on the circumstances, it can work for many adopted families who adopt from foster care.

10. Look for Opportunities to Build Resiliency in Your Fostered or Adopted Child or Teen

Tough times are often the times when children learn the most about themselves. Help your child take a look at how whatever they are facing can teach them "what they are made of." This is what resiliency is all about, teaching a child that they can survive the toughest of times and come out on top.

Parents and professionals working with fostered and adopted children play a substantial role in the development of resiliency in children. Here are a few helpful tips from Coulson (2013) that help kids bounce back.

1. Listening is one of the most important ways that we can build resiliency. Rather than operating on 'auto-parent' we will help our children know they are important by giving them our undivided attention. Children feel validated and worthy when we listen to them. While children are upset, sensitive listening provides emotional first aid. Listening with your heart allows you to be empathic, take your child's perspective or see the world through their eyes… giving advice when children are upset just makes them feel frustrated, or foolish. Coulson suggests that when your child tells you he is sad, you should try not to respond with "You can get over it." Instead, help your child to question his self-worth and realize that what he is feeling is normal based upon the situation. Try to avoid lecturing and instead reflect his emotions. Try saying, "I can see that you had a hard day at school" or "That experience must have made you feel very sad."

Instead, reflect their emotions and avoid advice or lectures.

"I can see it's been a tough day for you today."

"Wow, that must have made you feel really disappointed."

When they know you understand them, ask them how they think you can help. Let them strategize the most effective way to overcome their challenges and support them in their decisions or guide them toward appropriate actions...

2. Your child is likely to be resilient if they feel accepted for who they are. To really accept our children for who they are we must resist the temptation to judge and criticize. Continual fault-finding is a sure-fire way to create questions about self-worth in children. Additionally, children who are consistently criticized will start to wonder about their relevance.

In contrast, children whose parents affirm their children's efforts feel useful. When children are validated they feel worthy and acceptable as people. And they are also likely to work hard to maintain those positive feelings, which means when they encounter setbacks they will have the confidence to try again.

Letting children know specifically what you love about them or why you are proud of them can bolster resiliency... "You worked so hard at that activity today. I know you didn't come first, but all that matters is that you tried hard—and it looked to me like you gave it everything you had!"

Remember to be specific in your responses to your child. Try to avoid general phrases such as, "You're a great kid!" This kind of phrasing lacks specific meaning for the child. Instead say, John, you are great at painting." When we encourage our children based on their unique talents, they feel accepted by us.

3. One of the best things for promoting resiliency is a belief that we are competent and able to complete difficult challenges. Parents who identify their children's strengths and help them develop those strengths will see their children become increasingly competent. Their children will experience success. They will be inspired and confident. They will gain a sense that they have something to offer the world... Your child may possess strengths in relationships, academics, music, sport, creativity, curiosity or any number of other areas. By developing those strengths, inspiration, competence, and confidence will build resiliency in your child.

4. When you make a mistake, what do you do? Are you likely to throw your hands in the air and say it's too hard? Do you give up and go back to what you know you can do? Or do you see the mistake as a chance to learn something new, and try again?

    When your children make a mistake, what do they do? And perhaps more importantly, what do you say to them?

    When we try to help our children learn new behaviors we see setbacks and failures as opportunities for mastery. By teaching our children that continued effort, practice and learning are the keys to success, setbacks are no longer seen as frightening, and children become more resilient— willing to take risks and try new things.

    They are also more likely to look forward to possibilities in the future and have a more optimistic and curious nature. This mindset is strongly linked to resilience... Children will make lots of mistakes, even when trying their best. When our children do things that are wrong, we can focus on teaching them rather than punishing them. Often the most effective way to teach is to invite our children to think about what they have learned from a particular situation. We can then ask them to make decisions about the most appropriate course of action, such as apologizing, making restitution and refraining from doing what they have done again in the future.

Children who are resilient do better than children who are not resilient. Their parents use the skills outlined above to foster resiliency, and as a result resilient children:

- feel special and appreciated

- learn to set realistic goals

- have appropriate expectations of themselves and others

- believe they can solve problems and make good decisions

- see weaknesses as a chance to learn and do things better

- recognize, develop and enjoy their strengths and talents

- believe they are competent

- are comfortable with others

- have good interpersonal skills

- and most of all, resilient kids bounce back!

Resiliency Journey

Developing resiliency is a personal journey and you should use your knowledge of your children to guide them on their journey. An approach to building resiliency that works for you or your child might not work for someone else. If your child seems stuck or overwhelmed and unable to use the tips listed above, you may want to consider talking to someone who can help, such as a psychologist or other mental health professional.

Building resiliency with a fostered or adopted child or teen is an ongoing process that takes patience, dedication and a great deal of trial and error. However, with your continued support and dedication to your relationship with your child, you will experience positive change within your relationship. Remember that in the beginning many foster children are expecting you to give up on them. They will test you left and right, trying to push you away at every chance they get. This is your big chance to show them the true nature of "resiliency" by showing them through your actions that you will hang in with them through the hard times. Yes, this means through the times when they curse at you, or say they hate you or (my favorite saying): "You are not my real parents." It is very easy for anyone to invest more of themselves into a relationship with a child who is receptive to their overtures. We all know this. Life, however, is not always peaches and cream. Let's face it, relationships with friends, family and children are not either. People who are able to maintain their relationships with others for an extended period of time have one thing going for each other and that is "respect" for one another. This respect applies to when a person is going through a traumatic time and in good times. Please do not go through your life being a fair weather friend or parent. The healthiest people in this world are the ones who face struggles head on, move through them by doing what they need to do to get to the other side. This is what foster children need to be encouraged to do every day of their lives. They also need to be shown the respect they deserve in terms of their angry outbursts. Yes, I said respect for outbursts. Keep in mind that foster children's outbursts are a symptom of their inability to express verbally their fear of abandonment and rejection by you. Even though you may have no intention of rejecting the child, they do not know that and are living in fear of it. So, I am asking you to respect that this is where they are in their process of healing. Acknowledge that their disrespect is upsetting to you but also acknowledge that you understand where it is coming from. A big part of building resiliency is accepting one's faults. You can teach your fostered or adopted child this by accepting theirs. These children are not perfect, nor is any person, including yourself. We all have flaws.

I cannot say this often enough: as a professional or a parent of fostered or adopted children, you must show the child ongoing respect for their feelings about their trauma. One parent who has an amazing relationship with her adopted foster child told me, "We had to just let her go through her anger towards her biological parents and towards us. We let her do this as long as she did not hurt herself, us or others. We let her do this supporting her from a distance and, over time, the lashing out behaviors dissipated on their own. If we would have punished her for her actions, we just figured she would be more upset with us and we did not want that."

Every child who has been through trauma really does want to be loved and cared for, but they just do not have the first clue of how this works. How would they when many fostered or adopted children come from less than ideal parenting situations. Knowing this, there are several techniques you can implement with your fostered or adopted child along the way to demonstrate respect for their emotional trauma. The suggestions I am about to give you are from a former foster child named Jackie Hammers-Crowell. Jackie granted me permission to share with you her advice to in foster parents. Here is her true story.

I joined my first foster family at age eight. By then I had a pretty good idea of who I was and where I came from. I could tell my foster parents a lot of things about myself and my experiences. At the same time, though, there were things I could not tell them, either because I did not know or because I was afraid to speak up. Now that I am an adult,

I would like to share some things I wish my foster parents had known.

- You cannot and do not need to replace the parents who came before you. My birth mom and each of my foster parents hold unique places in my heart, even to this day. The foster parents of my second placement, who took me back for my sixth placement, earned the special title of Mom and Dad by being there for me and parenting the best they could with what they knew at the time. They were not perfect, but they loved me and never tried to compete with my mom.

- Do not break a child's spirit just to make her more docile. The outspoken nature of some foster children is a sign of intelligence and confidence, and they will need these tools to make it through foster care emotionally intact. At some point in time, children may have to advocate for themselves because of incompetent professionals or abusive adults in their lives. One thing I could have used as I tried to leave a bad placement at 15 was the big mouth I had at ten. Unfortunately, it took me years to get back to that level of self-advocacy after being taught that I would get along better if I just kept my mouth shut.

- Foster kids think about moving all the time. If they are happy, they worry that they will be moved. If they are unhappy, they think about asking to be moved or running away. When I was in care, I felt that everything was contingent upon where I would be when things happened. For example, I never let myself get excited about family vacations until just before they happened because in the back of my mind I knew I might move by then.

- Children have opinions about services they receive. Listen to what they say, even if you do not agree. If a child says he does not like his in-home therapist, find out why. The child may have a valid complaint. I once had a psychologist who fell asleep during sessions, but no one listened when I said I did not want to go to appointments until my foster dad witnessed one of the catnaps for himself.

- Foster children are who they are. Forcing children to be like you or someone else in your family offends them and suppresses greatness they already possess. Instead of trying to turn a child into someone else and being disappointed when it does not work, encourage each child to be—and be proud of—the best person he or she can be. One of the ways my foster parents did this was to tell me how smart I was and that I could go to college if I wanted. Though they would have liked me to get into sports, they learned that I was a brainiac and came to embrace that.

- Children need to identify talents and be something special. Help them find what they are good at and reassure them that they can keep doing it even if they leave your home. As a foster child, my biggest fear was not that I would be good at something, but that I would be good at it and then have to move to a family who would not let me do what I loved. One of the greatest services anyone ever did for me was to point out my talent as a writer. It was a gift no one could take away or stop me from developing.

- Kids who live in a foster home together become close. Denying a child the opportunity to see their foster siblings is one of the most hurtful things a foster parent can do. There is seldom an excuse for it and when it happened to me I felt the foster parents were only trying to hurt me. Consequently, I chose to never have contact with those parents again.

- Your foster child is just a kid and kids will make mistakes. Like all children, foster kids need to know that you will still love them when they mess up. This does not mean there cannot be consequences; it just means you will forgive them. Never assume they know this. Even after ten years and dozens of trials, it is always good to hear it again.

- After foster children leave, they will not forget you or anything that happened in your home. If you loved a child and gave her good memories, she will recall that later. By the same token, if you hurt a child do not expect that he will forget and be unfazed by it later. Childhood memories follow us all and shape who we are as adults. This is no different for children in foster care.

- When foster children become adults, they are not under your control anymore. The things you teach them in the meantime, however, are crucial. While it is important to teach your foster children practical things like how to keep a clean home and manage money, it is more important still to convey lessons about accountability, forgiveness, love and respect. You can do that by being accountable for your own actions, forgiving their mistakes and showing them— and the rest of your family—love and respect.

Though every foster parent I lived with made his or her share of mistakes, I am grateful each day that they chose to become foster parents. Had I not had places to call home or people who facilitated good medical care and encouraged me to pursue good grades, I might never have finished high school, let alone gone on to college and earned a degree. I want to thank every foster parent who reads this for continuing to suffer the heartache that goes along with helping children in foster care. As one of those children, let me just say that your efforts can make a world of difference.

(Hammers-Crowell, 2005)

Jackie Hammers-Crowell's experience is proof that foster children can succeed at what they want to do as she went on to a have very successful journalism career. Hammers-Crowell is one of many former foster children who have turned their trauma into success.

Fostered and adopted children who have been traumatized can become extremely resilient given the opportunity to build inner strength. I am asking you to be their guides and help lead them to success by (1) acknowledging that they are children of trauma who need you to see them through the storm and (2) putting the child's needs before your own. After all, isn't that what all parents should do to build resilient children whether they have experienced trauma or not?

Teaching Fostered and Adopted Children Self-Determination

In my opinion, self-determination is believing you can control your own destiny. That is what I want every fostered or adopted child and teen to know!

There are different theories about how to provide treatment to children who have suffered from trauma. I am from the school of thinking that supports helping children to see that trauma does not have to affect them for the rest of their life. With that being said, I do not mean to minimize that fact that abuse is serious because it is very serious and life altering. Most people agree however that violence at home can help create negative expectations and assumptions. Such children may have a diminished sense of self-worth and feel incapable of having a positive impact on the outside world. Hopelessness, self-blame and lack of control are typical of the feelings that can result from trauma; these feelings may lead to overwhelming despair and a loss of the ability to imagine the future or hope that circumstances will change.

> Many children exposed to violence view the world as a threatening place, in which danger and pain are to be expected. They see the world not through rose-colored glasses, but through a lens tinted somber gray. Children in an abusive environment develop extraordinary abilities to scan for warning signs of attack. They become minutely attuned to their abusers' inner states. They learn to recognize subtle changes in facial expression, voice, and body language as signals of anger, sexual arousal, intoxication, or dissociation. Children traumatized by family violence rarely understand that they see the world in a different way than their nontraumatized peers and teachers do. Traumatized children cannot simply remove their "trauma glasses" as they go between home and school, from dangerous place to safe place. They may anticipate that certain experiences and places are dangerous and anticipate them as being threatening. Due to this assessment, the child may avoid positive redirection.

According to the U.S. Department of Human Services (2013), the presence of emotional and psychological problems among many maltreated children is well documented. Clinicians and researchers report behaviors that range from passive and withdrawn to active and aggressive. Physically and sexually abused children often exhibit both internalizing and externalizing problems. Emotional and psychosocial problems identified among individuals who were maltreated as children include:

- low self-esteem

- depression and anxiety

- post-traumatic stress disorder (PTSD)

- attachment difficulties

- eating disorders

- poor peer relations

- self-injurious behavior (e.g. suicide attempts).

(U.S. Department of Human Services, 2013)

Maltreated children who developed insecure attachments to caregivers may become more mistrustful of others and less ready to learn from adults. They may also experience difficulties in understanding the emotions of others, regulating their own emotions, and in forming and maintaining relationships with peers.

One aspect of my treatment with abused and neglected fostered and adopted children that I do not think many clinicians focus on is teaching these children and teens the concept of self-determination. Self-determination is, I have found, a key concept in increasing these children's and teens' self-esteem. It also helps them to maintain their self-esteem throughout their lifetime. When a fostered or adopted child has finished treatment with me, I want them to walk out the door with:

1. positive self-esteem

2. self-determination.

Most importantly, I want these amazing strong children to know that their abuse does not define who they are. Children often feel or are told that they are to blame for their own maltreatment and for bringing "trouble" to the family; therefore, it is important to reassure children that they are not at fault (U.S. Department of Human Services, 2013). As I have said before, the abuse is and will always be a part of who they are; however, it does not define their existence. If a foster or adopted child or teen gets stuck there, then they will have a very difficult time moving forward with their dreams and their lives.

I want to share a brief story with you about a 13-year-old young man whom I treated for severe emotional and physical abuse. He was placed into the foster care system at age nine. In this story, I want you to focus on how determined this young man became to have a positive future despite his horrific upbringing.

Drew was a nine-year-old boy when he was placed into the foster care system because of severe abuse. I began to treat him at the age of 13. His father locked him in a freezer for 15 minutes when he was misbehaving. When I first met Drew he was quiet and meek. He would state, "I am bad and no good and nobody will ever want to be with me." Drew had no idea who he was or that he had potential to be anything but an abused young boy who did not deserve to be loved. He would state that, "I deserved what my dad did to me. I was bad." I simply asked Drew, "Do you know you have choices in this life? You have the choice to think that you are bad for the rest of your life or think that you can become a better person than your father told you you were." He suddenly became quiet and then said, "No one ever said anything like that to me before." "Well, they should have," I replied. I further stated that everyone has a choice to make something of their life. It is called self-determination. "Furthermore," I said, "No one, not even your own parents, has a right to hurt you or tell you that you can't do something. How do they know you can't if you never tried? Do not, Drew, let your father or the abuse that you suffered define who you are or will become. You define you!"

Many years later, I received an email from this young man and what it read was, "You define you. Dr. Sue, I want you to know that you helped me to define me."

Some professionals or parents may say that I am too direct with fostered or adopted children at times. I have also been told that my language can be too adult for them to understand. That is someone's opinion and I respect it. I also know that I have had to light a fire under every child I have worked with over the years to get them moving towards success and high self-esteem. I also know from my results of seeing these children build high self-esteem that it works.

Fostered and adopted children and teens are *not* "damaged goods." I have never thought of these children as such and I never will. I have found that professionals and parents who do view these children in this way hold them back from moving forward. They hold back their self-determination. I do not want to do that with these children. Seeing someone as damaged is saying, "They will never heal or have a life for themselves." I feel that fostered or adopted children have been held back enough from healthy attachments and positive relationships. I want them to know that despite what they have been through, they can be strong confident individuals and have positive relationships with others. If I see them as damaged goods, I am holding them back from reaching whatever their potential will be. Their biological parents did that to them. Please do not make the same mistake! Teach these children that they can become leaders, that they are loveable and capable of giving love. Teach them self-determination. If you do, you will be giving them not only self-confidence but self-love!

The skill of self-determination is critically important to help fostered and adopted children develop self-esteem because they often see themselves as failing when it comes to accomplishments. Due to their false negative perception of themselves, they often lack the self-confidence and determination to take chances. Who can blame them when they expect a result of rejection every corner they turn based on their initial feelings of rejection by their biological parents? I was constantly told by fostered and adopted children, "I can't try because I will just be disappointed or I would rather not try because I will just end up failing." First of all, I do not accept the word "can't" because to me it means "won't." I want fostered and adopted children to know they *can* at all times. I want them to know that their prior life circumstances do not have to dictate their futures.

Teaching a fostered or adopted child the key concept of self-determination helps the child to believe that they have the ability to accomplish personal and academic goals. Self-determination also gives the child courage to face their fears which leads them to the highest self-esteem and the ability to reach their full potential.

The capabilities needed to become determined are most effectively learned through real-world experience, which involves taking risks, making mistakes and reflecting on outcomes. These experiences help a young person test their strengths and limitations and identify appropriate short- and long-term goals (Bremer, Kachgal and Schoeller, 2003).

Fostered and adopted children need specific goals to reach for in order to build self-determination. These goals can be as simple as putting their clothes away each day. When simple goals are mastered, you can then move on to more challenging goals. First, the child has to know that they have the confidence to master more difficult goals. That will develop for them, once they are encouraged and praised for accomplishing the small goals. Something else to consider is that in order to take responsibility for their own futures, fostered or adopted children and teens need to know themselves and understand how their trauma and past experiences might affect their academic learning and relationships. With this knowledge, children are better able to develop plans, make decisions and learn from experience.

I have always been a proponent of explaining to a fostered or adopted child or teen that they may not be able to focus as well as they might on tasks because their mind might be focused on other areas of their lives such as not living with their biological family members or the worry of whether they will ever see their family again. I am always so perplexed when parents and professionals working with fostered or adopted children say, "The child is not doing well in school. I just don't understand it. The child is away from their parents and is safe." The child may be away from their parents physically, but emotionally the parents remain alive within the child's mind. I remember a 14-year-old adopted child telling me:

> I couldn't focus on anything in class. My mind was daydreaming all of the time about going home to my mother who would be clean and sober… I wished she would still come get me even though I was adopted…didn't she care about me?… I was angry and frustrated all the time… I couldn't focus on anything… I tuned the teacher's voice out all the time… I just wanted to be like everyone else.

As you can see, many fostered or adopted children often obsess on a daily basis about the trauma and abuse they have suffered prior to coming into care. You would too, if you had suffered in the way that these children have. You would not be able to focus in school or even focus on tasks that are asked of you. I always encourage foster and adoptive parents not to place judgment on the children but rather to be determined to gain a deep understanding of why they are experiencing the behaviors they are exhibiting. Your unconditional support is what helps and guides the child to build the self-determination to overcome their trauma.

So, how can you, the professional, foster parent or adoptive parent, help to build self-determination within a fostered or adopted child?

Here are some effective tips to guide you in the process (Bremer *et al.*, 2003):

- Promote choice making.

  - Identify strengths, interests and learning styles.

  - Provide choices about clothing, social activities, family events and methods of learning new information.

  - Involve children and young people in self-determination/self-advocacy opportunities in school, home and community.

  - Prepare children and young people for school meetings.

  - Speak directly to children and young people.

  - Involve children and young people in educational, medical and family decisions.

  - Allow for mistakes and natural consequences.

  - Listen often to children and young people.

- Encourage exploration of possibilities.

  - Promote exploration of the world every day.

  - Talk about future family lifestyles.

  - Develop personal collages/scrap books based on interests and goals.

- Promote reasonable risk taking.

  - Build safety nets through family members, friends, schools and others.

  - Develop skills in problem solving.

  - Develop skills in evaluating consequences.

- Encourage problem solving.

  - Teach problem-solving skills.

  - Accept problems as part of healthy development.

  - Hold family meetings to identify problems at home and in the community.

- Promote self-advocacy.

  - Encourage communication and self-representation.

  - Praise all efforts of assertiveness and problem solving.

  - Develop opportunities at home and in school for self-advocacy.

  - Provide opportunities for leadership roles at home and in school.

- Facilitate development of self-esteem.

  - Create a sense of belonging within schools and communities.

  - Provide experiences for children and young people to use their talents.

  - Provide opportunities to young people for contributing to their families, schools and communities.

  - Provide opportunities for individuality and independence.

  - Identify caring adult mentors at home, school, church or in the community.

  - Model a sense of self-esteem and self-confidence.

- Promote vulnerability.

  ○ This means allowing children to be vulnerable and express their feelings with you. As many of these children have been traumatized, they often shut down their feelings thinking that they will not be honored or just told to "get over it." Fear of not being accepted or listened to can cause low self-esteem. Being heard and comforted while sharing feelings increases self-esteem because it is showing the child that you acknowledge what they are saying. A simple response when they are sharing personal information with you about their past is: "Thank you for sharing that with me. Would you like me to respond to you?" If they say, "Yes," respond to the child. If the child says, "No," revisit it later. One thing that you must do is show them respect to gain respect. Remember what I said at the beginning of the book: It's you that has to prove to the child that you are there for them unconditionally, not vice versa.

- Help fostered or adopted children form a proud identity.

  ○ Develop a process that is directed by the child or young person to develop their identity: Who are you? What do you want? What are your challenges and barriers? What supports do you need?

  ○ Direct children and young people to write an autobiography or a life book.

  ○ Talk about the young person's abilities.

  ○ Identify and utilize support systems for all people.

(Bremer *et al.*, 2003)

It is also important that you find the determination within yourself to guide your child to success. A nurturing home, in which children have stable attachments to adults and are treated with physical and emotional respect, generally instills a fundamentally affirmative self-image and view of the world as benevolent (De Bellis, 2005).

Motivation

Motivation is the desire to do things. If I was not motivated to help fostered and adopted children build a sense of self and determination to see beyond their trauma, then I certainly could not have helped so many children to do this. So, I am saying that motivation is your key factor in helping yourself through the process of building self-determination within yourself and in fostered and adopted children.

Let's look at the definition of motivation for a second. Motivation is a psychological feature that arouses an organism to act towards a desired goal and elicits, controls and sustains certain goal-directed behaviors. It can be considered a driving force: a psychological one that compels or reinforces an action toward a desired goal. Ask yourself these three questions.

1. Do I have a desire to help my fostered or adopted child have a successful future?

2. Do I believe that I have the inner motivation to guide this child towards healing from the abuse they have suffered?

3. Do I have the desire to give this child a better life than they received early on?

I hope that you answered "yes" to all of these questions. If you did, then you possess the motivation skills to help your child become self-determined to heal and become successful.

The parents and professionals who *never* quit on the child and understand the child's needs in overcoming their sadness, fears and anxiety are the parents and professionals who succeed in the foster and adoption process. Remember the kids are expecting you to quit on them. To succeed in building self-determination and self-esteem in these children you *must never quit!* Would you want someone to quit on you? I think not!

You have to believe that the child is worthy of a better life. You have to believe that the abuse the child has suffered does not have to affect who they are for the rest of their lives. Most of all, you must believe that you have the power to guide the child on this journey to self-determination and a belief that the child can be more than a neglected, abused foster child. What this boils down to, in simple terms, is you being the force behind the child's healing process. If that means that you have to make sacrifices in your own life to do so, then that is what has to be done. As a parent to my own children, I make sacrifices every single day. That is what positive healthy parenting is all about. If you expect that a traumatized child, in this case, a fostered or adopted child, is simply going to come into your life without you having to do serious work on yourself to learn how to help the child, then you are not cut out to foster or adopt a child.

If you are not motivated to do everything in your power to help this child succeed then the child will not succeed. If you cannot give unconditional positive regard to the child, then the child will not succeed. Fostered and adopted children need *you* and your emotional and physical presence to succeed.

To make this process easier for yourself:

1. Sit down and make a list of the issues that you want to help your fostered or adopted child overcome.

2. Get a journal and write down your frustrations every day about what you are struggling with in terms of not being able to reach the child. Journaling helps you to release

your frustrations in a healthy way instead of directly on the child.

3. Take care of yourself. If you are feeling stressed, which will happen when caring for fostered or adopted children, take a break. The worst thing you can do, and this is where I see the relationship between the child and foster or adoptive parent go wrong, is when the parent becomes so stressed about not being able to help the child, anger erupts. Please be kind to yourself; this is not an easy process.

4. Seek professional help to manage your emotions if needed. I always say, "The healthiest people seek out therapy."

All of the tips above will, I hope, help you get determined and motivated. Your motivation and self-determination will help your fostered and adopted children gain determination and a desire to see that they deserve a good life!

Sense of Belonging

What is the one thing that most fostered or adopted children want? A sense of belonging to someone who will not give them away. I think that is what every fostered or adopted child wants and needs. If you think about it, isn't that what every person wants in life: to feel a part of something and somebody. It gives us proof that we actually matter in the world and lifts our self-esteem.

A sense of belonging increases children's self-esteem and gives them the confidence to want to be a part of other people's lives. Kim and Pellegrino (2012) suggest that:

Children sense that they belong by the way their parents talk to them and act toward them. Show and tell your child that you love and care for him or her. Children learn about how well they are doing by how their parents react to their behavior. Offer praise at least twice as often as you criticize.

Building a sense of belonging helps fostered and adopted children form a healthy identity. Remember that one of the main issues for fostered and adopted children is that they often feel as though they do not belong with anyone. How could they when the people who are supposed to care for them the most in life, their biological parents, rejected them? In my experience, you can tell an adopted child or foster child that their parents were not well enough to take care of them or that they wanted them to have a better life. The truth is that the kids do not hear it this way at all. The kids hear this as "I was not wanted." Our goal therefore as professionals and parents is to create an atmosphere where they can learn that they are wanted and worthy of being wanted. When an adopted or fostered child begins to feel they belong somewhere and to someone, they begin to feel positive about their identity.

I know that some of you might be thinking, "How can a foster child who is not in a permanent living situation feel a 'sense of belonging'?" If, for the time you spend with the child, you create and teach them a sense of belonging to your family, they will learn that it is possible to be a part of someone's life. The child then takes that sense of belonging with them for the rest of their lives. This leads back to what I was talking to you about earlier when we reviewed the "corrective emotional experience." The impact that you can make on a foster child's life while they are in your care can lead them very far in life. Adopted children, even though they may never have met their biological parents, often feel different from other children and that they do not belong, simply because they are adopted. They wonder about "not being wanted."

As parents and professionals of fostered and adopted children, you can create a sense of belonging by *including* fostered and adopted children within your family. I have highlighted the word including here because there are instances where I think some foster and adoptive parents do not understand what this term actually means. Please read the following two scenarios.

> Scenario 1: Mary was placed into a foster care home at age nine. The couple who agreed to foster Mary also have two biological children, both girls. When it comes to doing family activities, such as going to a movie, Mary's foster parents do not include Mary in the activities. They get a babysitter to stay with her while the "biological" family members go to the movies.

> Scenario 2: William was 14 when he was adopted by Mr. and Mrs. Petillo. Mr. and Mrs. Petillo also had two other children, one boy and one girl. When it was time for family vacation, William was so excited to go until he found out that he was not going. The Pettilos decided that only biological family members should attend.

These are two real-life examples of how children are not included within a family system. These are also two examples of how continued rejection of a child will only lead to continued low self-esteem. I treated both of these children in therapy. Both Mary and William were very angry and sad about not being included in activities or vacations. Their opinions about this were, "See, I told you nobody wants us." That is exactly the message that those two scenarios are sending to these children.

If you want to create a sense of belonging for fostered and adopted children, then you need first to recognize that for the time these children are with you, temporarily or permanently, it is your responsibility and job to create a sense of want and belonging. Here are some tips to make this happen. Remember, a sense of belonging creates high self-esteem in children.

- Let your child know that they are special: Find out what your child has passion for. Possibly it's art, music or sports.

When the child makes a great picture, or any picture for that matter, acknowledge it and say, "Great job."

- Praise your child but don't over-praise: Notice your child's strengths, even when they are misbehaving. Remember we all make mistakes. Praise the child when they accomplish moderate goals. Refrain praising the child for every accomplishment because it can become overkill and then doesn't mean anything. Fostered or adopted children may have difficulty with praise in the beginning but it will become more comfortable for them as they begin to receive it from different family members.

- Welcome the child into your home and your heart: For fostered or adopted children, belonging includes having a place in your home. Welcome the child into your home. Show them all the rooms in the house, especially their own. Say, "This is your room and I want you to feel comfortable in it. If there is something special that you would like in your room or a theme, we can talk about it together." I also like having something in their room with their name on it. It creates a sense of permanency for the time they are there. If you have rooms that are restricted in your house, then explain to the child why they are not allowed in there. If you make this a rule for your fostered or adopted child then it has to be a rule for all of the children in the house.

- One-on-one time: Showing a fostered or adopted child they belong in your family is showing them that they are important enough to have some alone time with you. I don't think there is anything more important than spending 10 to 20 minutes a day away from other family members and doing something one on one with the adopted child. It shows them that they are worthy of your time and your undivided attention. It also shows that they have a sense of belonging to the whole family and an individual connection with you.

- Don't force a connection: Expect rejection early on and try to accept it. I know it is hard to try very hard at something and feel rejected; however, if you have it in your mind that belongingness is somewhat foreign to these children then the feeling of rejection may not be so difficult to manage. All relationships take time to form and need to be built on trust. Go slow in the beginning.

- Create a family community: Try to include fostered and adopted children in your family decisions as much as possible. Ask their opinions about what movie to see and what restaurant to go for dinner. Have a family game night and stick to it.

- A place for everything: Anything labeled with the child's name speaks to permanency. Their shoe shelf, coat hook, special drawer, etc. will communicate the important message that not only are you important but your things are also valued here too! The same rule applies to bedroom signs and toothbrushes. We name our special items and spaces and keep them in places that are safe. So having household rules around respecting each others' privacy and belongings is especially important modeling for kids who may struggle with enjoying the moment instead of focusing on what will be purchased for them next (Fraser, 2009).

- Listen to your child:

  When a child is listened to it sends a message to the child that you care and value what they have to say. The more you listen and don't judge, the more attached the child will become to you. Don't ridicule or shame your child. Giving your child your full attention and truly listening to what he is saying and how he feels is an immediate self-esteem booster. When you turn off your phone, the TV and the computer and fully engage with your child it shows him that you really care about him and that you're interested in what he has to say. That kind of undivided attention is rarer than it should be these days and will make your child feel valued and loved. (Scheff, 2009)

- Set family rules: Family rules help children know that the family stands for something and gives them exposure to order and ritual. Have as few family rules as possible and enforce them consistently. Write down your family's rules and the consequences if those rules are broken (Kim and Pellegrino, 2012).

- Family meetings create cooperation and a sense of unity: Regular family meetings are a way to help children learn to cooperate. Fostered or adopted and biological children should be participating in these meetings. Family meetings are a place where family members discuss concerns and problems.

- Express appreciation: Let your fostered or adopted child know you appreciate their help with tasks, including household chores. If your child helps to clear the table, show them appreciation by telling them so. Appreciation is a key to belonging and high self-esteem. Materialistic objects do not always last forever but encouraging words do!

I know that you want to connect with your foster child or adopted child. I know that this is not always an easy process. I am a firm believer that anything worthwhile in life takes dedication and persistence. Building a healthy relationship with a fostered or adopted child or teen takes both. Families who are able to provide a strong sense of belonging for children reap some very positive results.

Generally, the values and habits of a group are transferred to the individual members of the group. In other words, members of a group tend to appreciate the same principles and ideas and perform all of the same routines and practices that the group does. So, if you create a sense that your fostered or adopted child or teen "belongs" to your family, they are likely to combine the values that you, as parents, model to them.

A sense of belonging helps fostered and adopted children make healthy decisions. It also helps them to know that if they mess up, there is someone in their life who will accept their mistakes. They usually are also better able to fight off loneliness and depression. Children who fear making mistakes usually do not have a positive sense of belonging in their family.

Children with a strong sense of belonging within their family see themselves as valuable, have self-respect and carry themselves with dignity and integrity. This translates to how they act outside the family, giving them confidence to make better decisions and participate in teams and other groups, as well as providing motivation to avoid risky behaviors. If they do not find their sense of belonging within their family, they will turn to other groups, which may not be positive, to satisfy this desire.

A sense of belonging gives everyone, including children, a sense of purpose. When a child feels there is a purpose to their existence, they have a desire to strive harder to meet goals. This in turn increases their sense of self-worth.

CHAPTER 8

Parenting an Adopted or Fostered Child or Teen

As a parent, you are the most important person in your child's life. Showing a child that they are important to you builds high self-esteem because it sends the message to the child that they have value. This goes for parenting biological children or fostered or adopted children. With that being said, I am fully aware that in the US state agencies inform foster parents not to get too "attached" to the child because there is a real chance the child will return to their biological family. As I have never gone much by the book in treating foster children, I just don't understand how a foster parent or therapist cannot get attached to these children. In fact, what do you tell a parent who has been fostering a child for two years or longer? Attachment is human nature and it is how people heal from trauma. If you are not attached, then I believe that you must look at yourself and find out why not. Also remember that experiencing loss is also a part of development and growth. Marriages break up, friendships do not always last and our loved ones leave sometimes. In therapy with foster children, I want to make a healthy attachment with each and every child, so they can take our relationship with them wherever they go in life. I know that I will not always be able to be there in person for them but I want to be with them in their mind and in their heart.

I learned just how important the development of attachment was from a foster child I worked with who was adopted. What I am about to tell you is a true story. It happened to me about a year ago as I was leaving Temple University in Philadelphia, PA where I teach psychology:

> I had my window down; it was a nice sunny day and one of my students called out, "Hey, Dr. Sue, have a great day." I stopped my car for a minute to say hello and she had her phone to her ear and on the line with her was a former foster child to whom I provided counseling ten years ago. I said to my student, "Who are you talking to?" She said, "Michael, from the Northeast Treatment Center" (*a place I worked providing therapy to foster children years ago*). "He knows you and says he will never forget you and that you changed his life." She then handed me the phone and it was Michael. I remembered him well. He was about ten years old when I met him. He had been through four foster homes and was abandoned by his biological mother; his siblings were put back with her but not Michael. He was a tiny kid who had dark brown eyes and light-colored skin. He did not talk much but when he did speak, he would ask, "Why did this happen to me?" Now, Michael was 19 years old and in college. I said hello on the phone and he replied, "Dr. Sue, is that you?" I said, "Sure is," and then blurted out, "This is random." He then said, "Not really, I always think about you and how you helped me through the worst times of my life. You made me believe in myself when no one did. I wouldn't be in college today or accepted my adopted family as my own if it wasn't for you. There was no one like you at that center and I'm glad I had you to help me. I am going to be a doctor, you know." I thanked Michael for all of the compliments and told him how proud I was of all of his accomplishments and to keep moving forward. I gave back the phone to my student

and then pulled away with tears in my eyes, repeating to myself "This is why I do my work with foster children." It was all very surreal but this experience is 100 percent true.

I did not share this story with you to toot my horn. I wanted you to know that it is because of all of the Michaels in this world that I believe that when you make a healthy connection with a fostered or adopted child you can lead them to high self-esteem and success. Most of this success begins and ends with you, the parents and the professionals who are in these children's lives. Remember, it's not how much time you spend with a child, it's how much understanding, dedication and patience you invest into your relationship with them. Saying goodbye is hard if and when it occurs, but please know that if you put in the effort with the child they will take all of your efforts with them wherever they go in their lives!

Your job as a foster or adoptive parent includes:

- building communication skills through listening and talking together

- using positive parenting to guide your child through life's ups and downs

- establishing a nurturing relationship built on love and trust

- acceptance that every day will bring challenges that you must learn to push through.

Research tells us that parenting styles can make a difference in a child's self-esteem. Better understanding on how to relate to your child are the basic tools all parents need to raise independent, confident, healthy and happy children (Baumrind, 1991; Maccoby, 1992).

Authoritative Parenting

To build resilient children, an authoritative parenting style is best. Authoritative parents:

- Listen to their children: My favorite saying to foster or adoptive parents is that we have to zip our lips and open our ears more. This is very difficult to do because, as adults, we want to help our children as much as possible; however, if we are running our mouths too much we are not listening. When we do not listen to a child, it sends a message that we are not acknowledging their voice.

- Encourage independence: A child needs to know you believe in them. It is not enough just to say it to a child, especially a foster child who has never had a great deal of encouragement. Even if you say it to the child in the beginning of your relationship, they probably will not believe you. With foster children, you have to gently encourage them towards independence. Brushing their teeth may even be hard to do by themselves. So, start out small and teach them to be independent by being their model. A word of advice: Do not expect the child to know basic independent skills when they come into your care or are adopted; encourage progress and do not expect it (Baumrind, 1991; Maccoby, 1992).

- Place limits, consequences and expectations on their children's behavior: I am often asked by foster or adoptive parents, "Should I discipline a foster child?" My answer is always the same, "Yes and you should also teach them that there are consequences for their behaviors." If a child does not have limitations set upon them, then they do not know how to exert self-control or self-regulate. Fostered or adopted children may resist limits at first, simply because they never had any placed on them. However, that does not mean that they should not be set for the child. Research demonstrates that children do best when there is proper structure (McLanahan and Sandefur, 1994). However, you must remember that extremely strict limits placed on a child do not encourage positive behaviors to occur. Simple limits in the beginning must be enforced and there must be room allowed for mistakes to be made by the child. For example, a foster child may have no idea what a "time out" means. They might just be used to being hit when they misbehaved prior to being placed in care which elicits a fear response. So, in the beginning, any form of punishment, even a time out may scare the child as well. I always like the approach of setting limits with traumatized children by first asking them why they did a certain behavior. Their answer may be "I don't know." That answer is perfectly okay. The child may really not know why they did what they did. With that being said, the child must still be told that the behavior is not acceptable and consequences can follow. That is how a child learns how not to repeat a behavior in a healthy way (Baumrind, 1991; Maccoby, 1992).

- Express warmth and nurturance: This is a key factor in building self-esteem in any child, but when it comes to fostered or adopted children, it is probably the most important factor you can give a child who needs to build resiliency. In order to have high self-esteem and self-acceptance, you must feel important and cared for. Remember that, in the beginning, a fostered or adopted child may reject your warmth and nurturance, simply because they did not receive a great deal in the past. Your best bet is to accept the rejection as a symptom of their history and keep providing the warmth and acceptance.

According to a study completed at the University of Minnesota by Mayek and Pitzer (2008), effective parental nurturing may be the single best predictor that a child will turn out successfully. Nurturing means giving our children the time, love, care, attention and affection they need to develop into competent and healthy adults. Nurturance builds self-esteem, develops attachment and allows children to be disciplined. Mayek and Pitzer suggest that in order to provide such love and nurturance parents need to:

- Provide real affection: Express unconditional positive feelings for your child.

- Love unconditionally: Children need to be accepted, trusted, even prized for who they are—our children—not for what they do. Acceptance means that when children don't behave you still love them, while letting them know you don't approve of the behavior. This love and acceptance gives children a sense of security, belonging and support. Show love through hugs, kisses or touch.

- Spend time together: Someone once said, "Children spell love T-I-M-E." Words of love are important, but they don't take the place of time spent with our children. Find things to do together such as reading, playing games or doing chores—something enjoyable for both of you.

- Really listen: When a child comes to you with a question or comment, stop what you are doing, look at the child and really listen. Your listening ear is more important to your child than your advice. Watch your children. What you see can help tell you how your children feel.

- Trust and respect each other: Encourage all family members to treat each other with respect. What children become has a great deal to do with the example set by those who raise them—parents who keep promises and who are honest and sincere. Fostered and adopted children need your guidance and patience to accept love. This is a process and one that can take a great deal of time. Feeling good about yourself does not occur overnight, but over time, from accomplishing goals and being complimented and valued for those accomplishments.

- Allow children to express opinions: When a child expresses an opinion and it is validated, a confident voice emerges for the child. In my early work with fostered and adopted children, I always emphasized how important their voice was to their healing. This, I felt, was very critical because their voice, if they had been living with abusive parents, was non-existent. They also did not have a voice in deciding where they would live after they were placed into foster care or if they were adopted. Having a voice means having the power to say what you feel and desire. When you have a voice and it is validated, you begin to use your voice more and gain confidence to use your voice in the future.

It is important for parents and professionals to guide a child's choices, but it is not acceptable to force one's opinions on a child. Parents and professionals should be able to direct children toward their future choices. Children have many interests and thoughts of their own which they wish to express. They are very conscious about themselves. Fostered or adopted children often struggle with the simplest of choices. This is often due to parental deprivation where language or early healthy interaction was limited. As I mentioned before, from my own experience you may ask a fostered or adopted child what their favorite color is and they may say, "I do not know." This presents a great opportunity to help them develop an opinion by simply asking, "Do you like green, blue, red, pink or orange?" This allows the child to make a simple choice and have an opinion.

Choices offered to young children must be legitimate and meaningful to them and acceptable to adults. Limiting choices for young children helps them select (Morrison, 1997). All human beings need to feel as if they have control over themselves and their lives. Kids need to feel this as well, especially to build positive self-esteem. In addition, they may feel hostility toward adults who allow them little freedom to choose (Edwards, 1993). Learning to be autonomous and self-reliant takes time and practice. When we offer children choices, we are allowing them to practice the skills of independence and responsibility, while we guard their health and safety by controlling and monitoring the options (Maxim, 1997).

People with authoritative parenting styles want their children to utilize reasoning and work independently, but they also have high expectations for their children. When children break the rules, they are disciplined in a fair and consistent manner. Authoritative parents are also flexible. If there are extenuating circumstances, they will allow the child to explain what happened and adjust their response accordingly.

The Effects of the Authoritative Parenting Style

Child development experts generally identify the authoritative parenting style as the "best" approach to parenting. Children raised by authoritative parents tend to be more capable, happy and successful. According to Baumrind (1991), children of authoritative parents:

- tend to have happier dispositions

- have good emotional control and regulation

- develop good social skills

- are self-confident about their abilities to learn new skills.

(pp.72–73)

Understanding Why Authoritative Parenting Works

Because authoritative parents act as role models and exhibit the same behaviors they expect from their children, kids are more likely to internalize these behaviors. Consistent rules and discipline allow children to know what to expect.

Because parents exhibit good emotional understanding and control, children also learn to manage their own emotions and learn to understand others as well. Authoritative parents also allow children to act independently, which teaches kids that they are capable of accomplishing things on their own, helping to foster strong self-esteem and self-confidence (Baumrind, 1967).

Authoritarian Parenting

Baumrind (1967) also discusses authoritarian parenting. Authoritarian parents have high expectations of their children and have very strict rules that they expect to be followed unconditionally. According to Baumrind, these parents "are obedience- and status-oriented, and expect their orders to be obeyed without explanation." People with this parenting style often utilize punishment rather than discipline, but are not willing or able to explain the reasoning behind their rules.

Characteristics of the Authoritarian Parenting Style

Authoritarian parents:

- have strict rules and expectations

- are very demanding, but not responsive

- don't express much warmth or nurturing

- utilize punishments with little or no explanation

- don't give children choices or options.

The Effects of the Authoritarian Parenting Style

Parenting styles have been associated with a variety of child outcomes relating to their social skills and academic performance. The children of authoritarian parents:

- tend to associate obedience and success with love

- may display more aggressive behavior outside the home

- may be fearful or extremely shy around others

- often have lower self-esteem

- often have difficulty in social situations.

I am not a proponent of authoritarian parenting when it comes to helping a fostered or adopted child or teen form high self-esteem. The reason for this is because very strict forms of parenting often resemble continued "abuse" to a child. The last thing that you want in helping a fostered or adopted child build self-confidence is to cause fear within them. Children of authoritarian parents are prone to committing rebellious acts as their way of asserting their individuality and finding their niche in the society.

Children who are raised in authoritarian households, in my opinion, are raised with black-and-white thinking. This often hinders a child from growing and learning that mistakes are made. This approach to parenting can also cause a child to have depression and damage a child's self-esteem.

Dr. Laura Markhan (2012) discusses the dangers to children's development when authoritarian discipline is used. She believes that:

1. Strict parenting deprives kids of the opportunity to internalize self-discipline and responsibility. Harsh limits may temporarily control behavior, but they don't help a child learn to self-regulate. Instead, harsh limits trigger a resistance to taking responsibility for themselves. There is no internal tool more valuable for kids than self-discipline, but it develops from the internalization of loving limits. No one likes to be controlled, so it's not surprising that kids reject limits that aren't empathic. They see the "locus of control" outside of themselves, rather than *wanting* to behave.

2. Authoritarian parenting—limits without empathy— is based on fear. It teaches kids to bully. Kids learn what they live and what you model, right? Well, if kids do what you want because they fear you, how is that different from bullying? If you yell, they'll yell. If you use force, they'll use force.

3. Kids raised with punitive discipline have tendencies toward anger and depression. That's because authoritarian child raising makes it clear to kids that part of them is not acceptable, and that parents aren't there to help them learn to cope and manage those difficult feelings that drive them to act out.

4. Kids raised with strict discipline learn that power is always right. They learn to obey, but they don't learn to think for themselves. Later in life, they won't question authority when they should. They're less likely to take responsibility for their actions and more willing to

follow the peer group, or to dodge responsibility by saying that they were only trying to "follow orders."

5. Kids raised with harsh discipline tend to be more rebellious. Studies show that children raised with a strict parenting style tend to be more angry and rebellious as teenagers and young adults. To see why, simply consider how this works for most adults. Virtually all of us were raised with some degree of harshness, and we chafe at control to that degree—even when we're the ones imposing it! That means we end up with problems regulating ourselves. Sometimes this shows up as anger and resentfulness at any perceived limit or criticism, or by over-reacting when we think someone is trying to tell us what to do. Sometimes it shows up in rebellion against the limits we impose on ourselves. For instance, we may harshly starve ourselves with a new diet and then rebel by binging. (Not surprisingly, studies show that kids raised with strict parenting are more likely to become overweight!)

6. Because kids raised strictly only "do right" when we're there, they get into more trouble. They also become excellent liars.

7. Authoritarian parenting undermines the parent–child relationship. Parents who relate punitively to their kids have to cut off their natural empathy for their children, which makes the relationship less satisfying to them. Parenting also becomes much harder for these parents because their kids lose interest in pleasing them and become much more difficult to manage. So strict parenting makes for unhappy parents. And children who are parented strictly end up fighting with parents and looking for love in all the wrong places.

The bottom line is that strictness does not work in creating better-behaved kids; in fact, it sabotages everything positive we do as parents and handicaps our kids in their efforts to develop emotional self-discipline.

Because authoritarian parents expect absolute obedience, children raised in such settings are typically very good at following rules. However, they may lack self-discipline. Unlike children raised by authoritative parents, children raised by authoritarian parents are not encouraged to explore and act independently, so they never really learn how to set their own limits and personal standards. While developmental experts agree that rules and boundaries are important for children to have, most believe that authoritarian parenting is too punitive and lacks the warmth, unconditional love and nurturing that children need (Baumrind, 1967).

It has been, and will always be, my belief that fostered and adopted children and teens need to be raised in an authoritative environment to build high self-esteem. We as professionals and parents can never recreate an environment that represents abuse in any way. All that environment creates for a child is continued anger, depression, fear and rebellion.

What You Give Your Child You Get

In his bestselling book, *Family First*, Dr. Phil McGraw (2004) talks about the concept of "what you give to a child you get." I am a big fan of this concept not only in relationships with children but also with adults. I often have parents seeking help from me who ask, "Why is my child so nasty to me? She curses at me and has no respect." My response to their question is usually, "How do you talk to your child? Do you raise your voice? Do you curse and yell when they do not respond?" I can tell you that nine out of ten times, parents respond by saying, "Yes, we yell, curse and scream because we don't know how to get through to the child." Well, then, "You get what you give." I stated before in this book that we must be our children's best role models. Yelling and cursing at a child is not being a positive role model. It is teaching a child that this is the way to be in life to get things done. If you are sending the child this message, then you should be prepared to take responsibility when they are fired from their jobs or disrespectful to authority figures. There is a great deal of truth in the old saying that "the apples don't fall far from the tree."

McGraw (2004) states that a parent's goal is to communicate, not dominate. He further points out that getting the point through to a child is more important than asserting control over the child. The act of control or being controlled by another person mostly causes a child to feel angry and resentful. This, in turn, can cause children to become rebellious.

This leads me to the term "reactive attachment disorder." This is a mental health disorder given to many abused or neglected fostered or adopted children by professionals when they cannot bond with their new foster or adoptive parents. You may not agree with all of my thoughts on this diagnosis but I feel the need to be as honest as I can be with you in this book.

Reactive attachment disorder (RAD) is defined as a condition where an individual has difficulty forming lasting relationships and lacks the ability to be genuinely affectionate toward others (Thomas, 2005). In addition, persons with RAD do not learn to trust others and do not appear to develop a conscience. This is believed to be caused by abuse or separation (physical or emotional) from one's primary caregiver during the first three years of life which translates to an internally suppressed rage. If untreated, children with RAD grow up to be adults who cannot truly ever feel love. It is suggested that many of these adults will eventually be labeled as sociopaths or psychopaths.

My overall concern with this label is not the fact that it is a diagnosis, it is the fact that I hear from many parents claiming that their fostered or adopted child cannot bond with them because they have RAD. A diagnosis of RAD should not be used as an excuse to stop trying to bond with the child. When I hear that response I just want to scream to parents, "Stop it! Do you hear what you are saying? Did you not realize that this child whom you decided to care for or adopt came from an environment where they did not have an opportunity to learn healthy attachment? They have no clue on how to attach to you or form a healthy parent–child relationship. Why are you pointing a finger at them? Look at yourself and how you are communicating and talking to this child. If you expect the child automatically to bond with you when you are expressing your frustrations to them about not attaching, you are headed for disaster. Please don't use the RAD diagnosis as an excuse for not being able to bond with your fostered or adopted child." It turns my stomach to hear anyone say, "My child has RAD and therefore I can't connect with them." It may be that the reason you cannot connect with the child is not the diagnosis; it may be because you are not communicating with the child in a healthy way and are letting your frustration from not reaching your goal stop you from learning and applying kind, accepting and healthy ways of parenting.

Foster children want to form healthy attachments to you and create a sense of belonging. However, they are not going to be able to accomplish that goal if they are being blamed for not knowing how to attach. High self-esteem in a fostered or adopted child is formed by teaching children to value themselves. How on earth will they learn to do this, if you do not value their prior experience (Kelly, 2011)?

If you are struggling to learn how to communicate effectively with your fostered or adopted child, you can learn how to do so. Here are some tips to get you started.

1. As with any new relationship, exchanges between foster parents and foster children can be strained. Foster parents can face a myriad of difficulties when trying to communicate

with their foster child. Foster parents often want to bond and share their world with their foster child. Although their intentions are well meant, foster parents can under-predict how untrusting and doubtful foster kids can be. Take the communication slow and know that sometimes a fostered or adopted child is communicating with you by kicking, screaming and yelling. This aggressive means of communicating can turn into healthier means of communicating over time.

2. There are lots of things that foster parents can do that will lend a sense of security to the foster child, and ease some of these communication challenges. Foster parents should be consistent; keep the same tone of voice during debates, maintain the same consequences, set clear roles and boundaries and stick with them. These can cultivate feelings of safety and predictability in the child, which in turn can lower the chances of running into these communication pitfalls (Kelly, 2011).

3. Other techniques that foster parents can utilize include slowing down communication and using simple language. Some foster children have experienced trauma around communicating, and may be vigilant to any cues that indicate that the situation is going to escalate. Foster parents may be trying to emphasize by raising their voice, or elaborating on a point. However, at times this can have an effect on the foster child which is the opposite of what was desired. They may hear and see the situation intensifying, which can spark anxiety, fear and sometimes anger. These intense feelings block the message the foster parent is trying to get across.

CHAPTER 9

The Triple Empowerment Self-Esteem System

Educate, Embrace and Empower

Educate

The "educational" stage of building self-esteem in fostered and adopted children begins with you taking personal steps in preparing and learning about how to create a safe environment for your children. If you have made the decision and the commitment to take on the role of becoming a foster parent or an adoptive parent, then I strongly encourage you to educate yourself about these children's symptoms of trauma prior to taking on the role of their caregiver.

Early intervention, to my mind, is the key to prevention. So, to empower and prepare yourself for your journey of parenting or working with fostered or adopted children and teens, please familiarize yourself with the psychological and behavioral issues that these children may experience prior to providing care. Learn about what I taught you in this book and then implement what was discussed about resiliency, building attachments, self-determination, motivation, belonging, unconditional positive regard and putting yourself in the child or teen's shoes. Your consistent implementation of these skills can only improve your relationship with your fostered or adopted child.

The parents and professionals whom I see having the most difficulty succeeding in the long run with their fostered or adopted children or teens are the individuals who think that love is enough to heal a fostered or adopted child or teen. This is a valid thought but, as I have said, not always reality based. Helping a fostered or adopted child or teen heal from trauma and build self-confidence also takes commitment, communication, acknowledgment, unconditional positive regard and self-sacrifice on your part. I encourage you to educate yourself on the emotional issues fostered and adopted children and teens experience before you make a full commitment to care for these children. Becoming a foster or adoptive parent should not be taken lightly. It is a very serious commitment that can be lifelong. If you decide to make the decision to care for these children after doing your "homework," I applaud you.

The information that I gave you in this book certainly does not cover everything that you need to know about fostering or adopting a child or teen. There are so many great resources on the internet today that can provide you with even more detailed information about working with fostered or adopted children. (They will be listed at the end of the book.) I also want to encourage you to speak to other foster parents who have fostered or adopted children. Ask them honest questions in regard to their opinions about the process and the ups and downs of parenting. Ask them what worked best in terms of building a healthy attachment with their foster children. Do not be afraid to ask the hard questions too such as, "Are you stressed a great deal?" "Do you feel as though you want to give up sometimes?" Ask what has helped them the most to press through the hard times. Do not forget either to ask about the positives of fostering or adopting a child, because there are a great deal of them. For example, one foster parent once shared with me that, "My experience of being a foster parent had its ups and downs but the joy of knowing and seeing that I could give this child some happy days when they didn't have many was the most rewarding experience I ever had." Educating yourself with other parents' knowledge and experience is a great way to prepare yourself for your journey with your children. In addition, it can be a very positive support system for you as well.

Raising an adopted child, being a foster parent or a professional helping a fostered or adopted child or teen to become successful is not a one-dimensional process. It takes many steps along the way to raise a confident successful child whether the child is biological, fostered or adopted. It is a process of twists and turns, just like any relationship. Teaching a child an "I can do" attitude takes great dedication on your part. If you can succeed in giving a fostered or adopted child or teen this attitude then you will be giving them a life of great possibility.

Another critical aspect of your education is to honestly take a personal inventory of your own self-esteem and make a decision as to whether you need to work on increasing self-worth. Every child who has high self-esteem has parents or someone in their lives who possess a high level of positive self-worth. Possessing a high level of self-worth provides every child with a great role model to observe which in turn helps them to build their own self-confidence. I could never do the self-esteem work with fostered or adopted kids if I did not have confidence within myself. The kids would see right through me and say, "Why is this person trying to help me to become confident when she is not confident herself?" There is nothing wrong with admitting that we need some help to make improvements to ourselves. In fact, the more improvements we make to ourselves as parents and professionals, the greater positive impact we can make on our children. So, if you know that you do not have the best self-image, make a commitment to seek out help to improve it. Your fostered or adopted children and teens will thank you for your efforts.

Education is empowerment. The more you know about the possibilities that may arise within your relationship with your fostered or adopted child, the better you will be able to manage a crisis when it arises.

Embrace

Now that you have equipped yourself with your educational tools, you are ready to embrace the fostered or adopted child or teen and make them a part of your life, family and community.

Embracing a fostered or adopted child or teen to me means unconditionally accepting that the child may mess up at times and make mistakes. Embracing also means not giving up on the child when things get difficult. For you, the parent or the professional, it means accepting that neither you nor the child or teen are perfect. You are going to make a great deal of mistakes along the way, as are the children. When we can accept that we have flaws, it gives us room to learn from our mistakes and try again. It also shows children that they do not have to be perfect either. We must give fostered and adopted children this respect as well. They may have been moving through life without a healthy or healing guiding force. We all need to be that healthy guiding force to lead them to personal success. We must embrace fostered and adopted children and teens emotionally and put ourselves in their shoes. We must join with them in their pain and empower them to move through their healing. We also want to accept where they are at the moment and believe that they will not be in that moment forever. We need to embrace them during crisis instead of running away. You need to give them corrective emotional experiences and they need to look to you as their positive role model for change.

Remember what I said at the beginning of the book: The two most important critical aspects of helping fostered and adopted children and teens are (1) helping them to form a healthy attachment and (2) building their self-esteem. I have not changed my mind about that. I also believe that a critical factor in embracing these children is creating a safe environment where trust can be built. You can accomplish this by listening, accepting, acknowledging and encouraging them to move beyond their fears.

As you have learned, forming an attachment to a child who has had a prior dysfunctional attachment to a caregiver is challenging but not impossible. You know that it takes time, patience and a great deal of effort on your part. You also now know that it can include "rejection" after "rejection" on the child's part towards you. If you are educated about these reactions before you encounter them, then you can embrace the child with this knowledge and be a bit more prepared for the hurt that you will feel when it happens. If you can realize that a fostered or adopted child or teen's reaction is just a way to protect themselves from further perceived rejection by another adult, you will be able to help them heal.

Empower

Gaining knowledge and understanding is part of empowerment. Self-empowerment means to gain knowledge and understanding of the self and take charge of your own life. When you take charge of your own life, you are much better prepared to influence other people's lives, including fostered or adopted children and teens.

If you take away one thing from this book, I want it to be that you believe that you have the power within yourself to make a positive difference in a fostered or adopted child or teen's life. If you truly believe this then you will create positive change within both your life and your child's.

To become that empowered force within a fostered or adopted child or teen's life, you have to incorporate all of the techniques that you have learned in this book into your daily life of parenting or working with fostered or adopted children.

As I said earlier, I have written this book to provide you with the empowerment and educational tools for working with or parenting these children or teens. Preparation, I have always felt, is empowerment. When one feels helpless, one can go into a panic mode and that is where things begin to fall apart. I see this a great deal with parents of adopted and fostered children who are not familiar with the symptoms of abuse or neglect prior to making a commitment to the child. We are all more powerful and effective parents and professionals when we have prepared ourselves for instances that could occur. Be that empowered parent or professional for fostered and adopted children and teens.

Self-empowerment is not simply thinking you can do something, it is knowing that you can. This is the positive attitude that you need to be a parent or a professional to a fostered or adopted child or teen.

Let me leave you with this. When I started providing outpatient therapy 15 years ago, I had to first educate myself on how to connect with abused and neglected foster children. I could not embrace these children until I accomplished that goal. It was a big struggle in the beginning. My supervisor was right when she reminded me as I walked out the door after our first interview that I would be challenged. I was challenged every single day I walked into work. One particular thing that I believe I did right, while working with these children, is that I never walked away from any child that I felt needed me. When I did not know how to help, I took it upon myself to learn how. I read books and spoke with specialists in foster care and adoption. I learned on the job. I tried different techniques at times to connect with the kids. What worked with one child did not always work with another child. I never gave up!

The most important lesson I learned over those six years of providing therapy at the foster care agency was that it was not the techniques that helped these children build trust with me and heal. It was the fact that they knew someone believed that they were more than just a fostered or adopted child. You can empower fostered and adopted children by showing them that you believe in them too.

The one thing that these amazing children have been most stripped of in life is a true sense of value and acknowledgment. As parents and professionals, we must make it our number one priority to empower fostered and adopted children and teens through acknowledging them every single day. It is what they most want, need and desire in order to have high self-esteem.

PARTING WORDS

If my mother had not run out of the house when I was eight years old, I do not think that I would be working with fostered and adopted children today. It's interesting how incidents in our lives affect our future. That night 32 years ago, I realized that I never wanted any child to feel the way that I did, wondering if my mother would ever return home. I am so grateful that she did.

Going to work and counseling fostered and adopted children never felt like work to me. It felt as though it was my purpose. On my last day at the agency in 2002, I saw one of the teenagers whom I had the pleasure to work with: the one who wrote the Foreword. For two years, we built a trusting safe relationship. She was a tough kid and sharing her feelings was the most difficult part of her healing. On that summer day in 2002, I handed her a letter. In the letter, I told her how proud I was of the young woman she had become. I admired her strength and her unrelenting desire to achieve success. As she walked out the door, she turned and handed me something that was wrapped in paper and said, "Don't open it until I go." I agreed. As the door closed, I sat down at my desk and opened the package. Inside was a picture of the two of us in a frame and a note inside that read:

To Dr. Sue,

I just wanted to have the chance to actually thank you for all that you have done for me. You taught me lessons that have helped me to succeed. You were a teacher, therapist and advocate for me. You are a true best friend. You were always there for me when I needed someone to talk to when I was down. You always made me see the light or positive in every situation. You could always make me laugh and smile no matter what kind of mood I was in. You will always be to me more than a therapist. You are a true friend.

Keep in touch

Nyleen

The picture Nyleen gave me that day has sat on my desk for the last 12 years. It reminds me every day of the importance of my work with fostered and adopted children. It gives me encouragement to know that these children can build high self-esteem and confidence because of a corrective healthy relationship.

Several years later, I received an email from Nyleen. She wanted to let me know that she had graduated from college. She also informed me that the letter I had written her in 2002 hung on her wall behind her bed ever since and that she reads it every morning to give her strength and confidence for the day. I was amazed and touched deeply by her gesture. Her actions confirmed exactly what I have believed to be true for years: that even though you cannot be in fostered and adopted children's lives every day as a professional in the field, you can be in their hearts and continue to guide them towards success.

I encourage you to be a fostered or adopted child's guide to a healthy and hopeful life of success. I know that you have the power within yourself to help these children succeed. Never lose sight of the fact that your fostered or adopted child's life is shaped by you being their best role model.

REFERENCES

Introduction

Child Welfare Information Gateway (2013) "Foster care statistics 2012." Available at https://www.childwelfare.gov/pubs/factsheets/foster.pdf, accessed on 20 May 2014.

Congressional Coalition on Adoption Institute (2014) "Facts and statistics." Available at http://www.ccainstitute.org/index.php?option=com_content&view=category&layout=blog&id=25&Itemid=43, accessed on 20 May 2014.

Chapter 3

Bowlby, J. (1973) *Attachment and Loss. Vol. II. Separation: Anxiety and Anger.* London: Penguin Books.

Bass, S., Shields, M.K. and Behrman, R.E. (2004) "Children, families, and foster care: Analysis and recommendations." *Children, Families, and Foster Care 14,* 1, 5–30.

Bowlby, J. (1990) *A Secure Base: Parent-Child Attachment and Healthy Human Development.* New York: Basic Books.

Chen, M. and Fan, X. (2001) "Parental involvement and students' academic achievement: A meta analysis." *Educational Psychology Review 13,* 1–22.

Committee on Integrating the Science of Early Childhood Development (2000), J.P. Shonkoff and D.A. Phillips (eds) *From Neurons to Neighborhoods: The Science of Early Childhood Development.* National Academic Press: Washington, DC.

Johnson, M. (2011) "What's your joy trigger?" Available at www.huffingtonpost.com/margaret-wheeler-johnson/joy-trigger-little-things-happiness_b_944661.html, accessed on 14 March 2014.

Levy, M.T. and Orlans, M. (1998) *Attachment, Trauma, and Healing: Understanding and Treating Attachment Disorder in Children and Families.* Child Welfare League of America.

Levy, M.T. and Orlans, M. (2014) *Attachment, Trauma, and Healing: Understanding and Treating Attachment Disorder in Children and Families (2nd Edition).* London: Jessica Kingsley Publishers.

Mueser, K.T., Rosenberg, S.D., Goodman, L.A. and Trumbetta, S.L. (2002) "Trauma, PTSD, and the course of severe mental illness: An interactive model." *Schizophrenia Research 53,* 123–143.

National Child Traumatic Stress Network (2013) "Early childhood trauma." Available at www.nctsn.org/trauma-types/early-childhood-trauma, accessed on 14 March 2014.

New, M. (reviewer) (2012) "The story on self-esteem." KidsHealth.org. Available at http://kidshealth.org/PageManager.jsp?dn=KidsHealth&lic=1&ps=307&cat_id=20680&article_set=22505, accessed on 14 March 2014.

Plummer, D.M. (2007) *Helping Children to Build Self-Esteem: A Photocopiable Activities Book (2nd Edition)*. London: Jessica Kingsley Publishers.

Ryan, M.R., Stiller, J.D. and Lynch, J.H. (1994) "Representations of relationships to teachers, parents and friends as predictors of academic motivation and self-esteem." *Journal of Early Adolescence 14*, 226–249.

Schecter-Cornbluth, S. (2006) *A Phenomenological Investigation of Foster Adolescents' Experiences of Being Separated from their Biological Parents*. Doctoral dissertation, Chestnut Hill College.

Sears, W. (2011) "12 ways to help your child build self-confidence." Ask Dr. Sears. Available at www.askdrsears.com/topics/parenting/child-rearing-and-development/12-ways-help-your-child-build-self-confidence, accessed on 14 March 2014.

Sroufe, L.A., Egeland, B., Carlson, E., and Collins, W.A. (2005) *The Development of the Person: The Minnesota Study of Risk and Adaptation from Birth to Adulthood*. New York: Guilford Press.

Chapter 4

Rogers, C. (1961) *On Becoming a Person*. Boston, MA: Houghton Mifflin.

Chapter 5

Cannon, B. (1994) "Walter Bradford Cannon: Reflections on the man and his contributions." *International Journal of Stress Management 1*, 20–35.

Chapter 6

Butler, G. and Hope, T. (2007) *Managing Your Mind: The Mental Fitness Guide*. New York: Oxford University Press.

Sears, W. (2011) "12 ways to help your child build self-confidence." Ask Dr. Sears. Available at www.askdrsears.com/topics/parenting/child-rearing-and-development/12-ways-help-your-child-build-self-confidence, accessed on 14 March 2014.

Chapter 7

Alvord, M.K., Gurwitch, R., Martin, J. and Palpmares, R.S. (2003) *Resiliency Guide for Parents and Teachers*. Washington, DC: American Psychological Association.

Bremer, C.D., Kachgal, M. and Schoeller, K. (2003) "Self determination: Supporting successful transition." *Research to Practice 2*, 20–30.

Coulson, J. (2013) "Teaching your children resiliency." Available at www.kidspot.com.au/schoolzone/Friendships-Teaching-your-child-resiliency+3994+394+article.htm, accessed on 14 March 2014.

De Bellis, M.D. (2005) "The psychobiology of neglect." *Child Maltreatment 10*, 2, 150–172.

Frazer, T. (2009) "How to foster a sense of belonging for foster children." Ontario Association of Children's Aid Societies, 54(4). Retreiced from http://www.oacas.org/pubs/oacas/journal/2009Fall/foster.html.

Hammers-Crowell, J. (2005) "My advice to foster parents." Available at www.adoptinfo-il. org/myadvice, accessed on 14 March 2014.

Integrated Child (2013) "The importance of giving your child choices." Available at http://integratedchild.com/the-importance-of-giving-your-child-choices, accessed on 14 March 2014.

Kim, S.K. and Pellegrino, L. (2010) "Growth and development: Helping your child build self-esteem." Available at www.webmd.com/parenting/helping-your-child-develop-healthy-self-esteem, accessed on 14 March 2014. *Adoptalk newsletter* (2005) North American Council on Adoptable Children.

Masten, A.S., Best, K.M. and Garmezy, N. (1990) "Resiliency and development: Contributions from the study of children who overcome adversity." *Development and Psychopathology 2*, 425–444.

Scheff, S. (2009) "Top 10 parenting quick tips of 2009." Available at www.education.com/ reference/article/Ref_Top_10_Parenting, accessed on 14 March 2014.

Sirota, M. (2010) "Moving beyond the victim role – taking personal responsibility." Available at http://ezinearticles.com/?Moving-Beyond-the-Victim-Role---Taking-Personal-Responsibility&id=4070204, accessed on 14 March 2014.

Sroufe, A. (1997) "Psychopathology as an outcome of development." *Development and Psychopathology 9*, 256.

Taylor, J. (2009) "Parenting: Decision making." The Power of Prime. The Cluttered Mind Uncluttered. *Psychology Today*. Available at www.psychologytoday.com/blog/the-power-prime/200910/parenting-decision-making, accessed on 14 March 2014.

U.S. Department of Human Services (2013) "Child welfare and neglect." Available at www. childwelfare.gov/pubs/usermanuals/foundation/foundationf.cfm, accessed on 14 March 2014.

Vachss, A. (1994) "You carry the cure in your own heart." *Parade Magazine*, 28 August.

Chapter 8

Baumrind, D. (1966) Effects of Authoritative Parental Control on Child Behavior, Child Development, 37 (4), 887–907.

Baumrind, D. (1991) "The influence of parenting style on adolescent competence and substance use." *Journal of Early Adolescence 11* (1), 56–95.

Edwards, D. (1995) Making choices about discipline. American Secondary Education 22 (2), 17–21.

Kelly, C. (2011) "Tips for communicating with your foster child." Available at http:// voices.yahoo.com/tips-communicating-foster-child-7703928.html?cat=25, accessed on 14 March 2014.

McGraw, P. (2004) *Family First*. New York: Free Press.

McLanahan, S.S. and Sandefur, G. (1994) *Growing Up with a Single Parent: What Hurts, What Helps*. Cambridge, MA: Harvard University Press.

Maccoby, E.E. (1992) "The role of parents in the socialization of children: An historical overview." *Developmental Psychology 28*, 1006–1017.

Mayek, B. and Pitzer, R.L. (2008) *Using Nurturance and Prevention Tools*. University of Minnesota Extension.

Maxim, G.W. (1997) *The Very Young: Developmental Education for the Early Years (5th Edition)*. Upper Saddle River, NJ: Merrill/Prentice Hall.

Morrison, G.S. (1997) *Fundamentals of Early Childhood Education*. Upper Saddle River, NJ: Merrill/Prentice Hall.

Thomas, L.N. (2005) *When Love is Not Enough: A Guide to Parenting Children with RAD – Reactive Attachment Disorder*. New York: Families By Design Inc.

RECOMMENDED RESOURCES

BOOKS

Cairns, K. (2002) *Attachment, Trauma and Resiliency: Therapeutic Caring for Children*. London: British Association for Adoption and Fostering.

Carter, C. (2011) *Raising Happiness: 10 Simple Steps for More Joyful Kids and Happier Parents*. New York: Ballantine Books.

Carter, D. (2007) *No Momma's Boy*. New York: iUniverse, Inc.

Cornbluth, S. (2006) *The Ambiguous Foster Child*. King George, VA: American Foster Care Resources.

DeGarmo, J. (2013) *The Foster Parenting Manual: A Practical Guide to Creating a Loving, Safe and Stable Home*. London: Jessica Kingsley Publishers.

Eldridge, S. (1999) *Twenty Things Adopted Kids Wish Their Adoptive Parents Knew*. Eldridge, NY: Delta.

Fahlberg, V. (2012) *A Child's Journey Through Placement*. London: Jessica Kingsley Publishers.

Hughes, D.A. (2006) *Building the Bonds of Attachment: Awakening Love in Deeply Troubled Children*. New York: Jason Aronson.

Kaufman Espeland, G. (2012) *Stick Up for Yourself! Every Kid's Guide to Personal Power and Positive Self-Esteem*. Minneapolis, MN: Free Spirit Publishing Inc.

Markhan, L. (2012) *Peaceful Parent, Happy Kids: How to Stop Yelling and Start Connecting*. New York: Penguin.

Mitchell, C. (2007) *Welcome Home, Forever Child: A Celebration of Children Adopted as Toddlers, Preschoolers, and Beyond*. Bloomington, IN: Author House.

Schooler, J.E., Keefer Smalley, B. and Callahan, T.J. (2012) *Wounded Children, Healing Homes: How Traumatized Children Impact Adoptive and Foster Families*. Carol Stream, IL: Tyndale House.

Toth, J.R. (1997) *Orphans of the Living: Stories of America's Children in Foster Care*. New York: Simon & Schuster.

Vardalos, N. (2013) *Instant Mom*. New York: Harper Collins.

INTERNET RESOURCES

Adopt Us Kids www.adoptuskids.org

Child Welfare Information Gateway (see "Adopting Children from Foster Care") www.childwelfare.gov/adoption/adoptive/foster_care.cfm

Dave Thomas Foundation for Adoption www.davethomasfoundation.org

Foster Care Alumni of America www.fostercarealumni.org

National Foster Parent Association www.nfpaonline.org

INDEX